savor

AMBER LOCKE

savor

SENSATIONAL SOUPS TO FULFILL & FORTIFY

MITCHELL BEAZLEY

CONTENTS

✳ Introduction   6

    About me   6
    About this book   6
    Why soup?   7
    Types of soup   7
    What makes a good soup?   8
    How to blend a soup   8
    Making, serving & storing tips   9
    Tool kit   10
    Finishing touches   12
    What makes a good stock?   14

✳ Soups   18

✳ Toppings & sprinkles   126

    Dry sprinkles   128
    Cooked sprinkles   132
    Drizzles   135
    Other stocks, sauces & liquids   138

✳ Index   140
✳ Acknowledgments   144

ABOUT ME

My love of fruit and vegetables stems from my childhood and growing up with enthusiastic gardeners as parents. We always had a huge vegetable garden at every house we lived in and a seemingly constant, year-round supply of seasonal fruit and vegetables. I remember the thrill of digging up new potatoes as a child. It felt like discovering treasure as I carefully unearthed the small golden-yellow tubers and piled them into a bucket with glee. I loved picking herbs, tomatoes, lettuce, raspberries, and peas in the summer, and gathering apples and plums from the orchard and dessert grapes from the vine in fall.

My parents would spend hours and hours tending the different vegetables, often growing them from seed, and the garden was always immaculately kept and beautiful to look at. Alongside their favorite fruit and vegetables would be new and experimental varieties such as rainbow chard, ornamental pumpkins, or, one year, Siberian, American, and cold-climate varieties of tomato.

My mother is also a great cook so not only did I grow up surrounded by a bounty of fresh produce, I was taught how to cook with it, too. One of her theories is that every meal should feature at least seven different colors for it to be properly healthy, so the food that she prepares is not only garden-fresh but super colorful, too. I guess some of her enthusiasm rubbed off on me.

My diet now is predominantly vegetable-based and I'm also a big raw food advocate and enthusiast. However, I do appreciate the merits of cooked vegetables too, especially the grounding and comforting role they can play in the colder fall and winter months. So soups and salads are the two types of dishes I most commonly eat.

The soup I remember most fondly from my childhood is celery soup, which my mother would make for me as a treat (see my Celery Soup version on page 76). I loved its natural creaminess when blended and its slightly salty, lemony flavor. When I was a little older, she'd serve it with crushed pink peppercorns, which

I thought was the height of sophistication aged ten. In more recent years, certain soups stick in my memory: a wild mushroom soup with the most amazing depth of flavor served at a local Derbyshire restaurant (see my Mixed Mushroom soup version on page 68); a beautiful fish bouillabaisse at La Residencia hotel in Mallorca; a fabulous onion soup at a French restaurant on a recent trip to New York; and even the super-quick tomato and rice soup that I frequently make when I'm pressed for time (see the totally raw, totally vegan version Tomato Cauli Rice Soup on page 51). All these soups, and many more, hold memories of my life.

ABOUT THIS BOOK

This book showcases my love of fruit and vegetables and one of my favorite ways to serve them—in colorful and nutritious soups.

The soups you will find here are all vegan—some raw, some cooked, and some sweet—but all come with alternative serving ideas, many of which will appeal to omnivores. You'll find a soup for every color of the rainbow, which illustrates the amazing and diverse spectrum of colors that occur naturally in nature and shows how easy it really can be to "eat—or drink—the rainbow."

I've also included staple recipes for base stocks, health information on ingredients, tips for storage and serving, kitchen kit advice, and a collection of toppings, drizzles, and sprinkles to perk up the look, taste, texture, and nutritional value of your soups.

So, in praise of fruit and vegetables, this book is a true celebration of their versatility, the vital role they play in our diets, and how they help us stay healthy. I hope you'll find plenty to entertain and inspire and that you, like me, also enjoy the beauty of soup.

Amber

WHY SOUP?

A humble bowl of soup is one of the most versatile of dishes; there's nothing quite like spooning up warm goodness on a cold winter's day, sipping a light chilled soup to refresh in the summer months, or hugging a mug of comforting broth if you're feeling under the weather. A simple bowl of soup has the ability to do far more than nourish the body; it has the restorative and comforting power to revive us and soothe the soul, too.

Whether served warm or chilled, as a snack or main meal, soups are readily adaptable. Most can be made more substantial with extra vegetables, added protein and carbs, or spruced up with a selection of interesting toppings—they're almost the little black dress equivalent of the culinary world.

Usually a healthy choice, soups are more often than not vegetable-based and provide a great opportunity to sneak in extra vegetables. I find a handful of finely grated raw carrot or zucchini stirred into a flavorsome soup just before serving can often go undetected. They're economical to make, too, and can be a wonderful way of using up odds and ends in the fridge, leftover cooked vegetables, or utilizing slightly wilted specimens that you might otherwise discard.

If you're watching your weight, soups can be your best friend in the kitchen because they quickly assuage hunger and leave you feeling satisfied for longer. A raw soup can be whipped up in minutes so is ideal if you're feeling ravenous, or if made in bulk and frozen in portions, a soup can take mere minutes to defrost and serve up. Similarly, if you crave something sweet, my recipes for low-sugar fresh fruit soups (see pages 112–125) are the perfect antidote.

TYPES OF SOUP

Gazpacho, chowder, mulligatawny, vichyssoise, borscht, velouté, pho, minestrone, broth, ramen, potage, bisque, and consommé are all names that can define the ingredients in a soup, its texture, style of cooking, and/or the country of origin. But what is clear is that soup comes in many guises to suit every eating occasion or mood. There are delicate, clear broths; rustic, chunky, soups-cum-stews; or silky-smooth versions with a velvety texture and creamy mouthfeel. Soups can be healthy, cleansing, and nourishing or luxurious and indulgent, as well as quick to prepare or cooked slowly over a long period of time. Whatever the type, all good soups start with some basic, fresh ingredients and a little know-how.

WHAT MAKES A GOOD SOUP?

As with any recipe, a good soup normally begins with good ingredients. For me, the following are key:

✳ FRUIT & VEGETABLES: I like to use organic fruit and vegetables whenever possible. These often have the best flavor and you don't need to peel them. Just scrub the vegetables, including beets, carrots, parsnips, sweet potatoes, and potatoes, clean before use. Keeping the skins on means you retain a lot of the nutrients. If you are using produce that is not organic, it's best to peel it first.

✳ COOKING OIL: I generally try to use as little additional oil as possible and when sautéing vegetables for a soup I'll often steam-fry them (see Making, Serving & Storing Tips opposite). My preferred oil is coconut since it has many health benefits and a high smoke point. The coconut flavor is normally undetectable, but for more delicately flavored soups I opt for a light olive oil.

✳ STOCK: I tend to use four basic types of stock (see pages 14–17). The Cooked Vegetable Stock is the one I go to for most soups and it's even delicious drunk on its own like a broth. For more delicately flavored soups I'll use the light vegetable stock, or when I want to add other flavorings or aromatics. If I'm making a Thai-style soup, for instance, I may add lemon grass, cilantro, or fresh ginger to the light stock, or include star anise to make a Chinese-inspired broth. The Dehydrated Vegetable Stock Powder is a great "instant" stock when in a hurry or to give a flavor boost to a soup, while the Raw Vegetable Stock is a must for raw soups and to give a fresh-tasting flavor boost to other types of soup, stews, and sauces.

✳ FINISHING TOUCHES: a few well chosen extras can make all the difference to a soup, boosting its nutritional value and transforming it into something special. Toppings don't have to be elaborate: a handful of sprouted seeds, crushed dry-roasted peanuts, or crunchy sourdough croûtons scattered over the top are often enough. A spoonful of grated carrot, a few chopped herbs, a drizzle of yogurt or cream, or a sprinkle of spices can all lift and enliven a bowl of soup. (See pages 128–139 for more ideas.)

HOW TO BLEND A SOUP

Of course, some soups, such as consommé, miso, or more chunky stewlike soups don't require blending, but I prefer to blend my soups. However, the method I use depends on the texture I want to achieve.

✳ My food processor gives a coarse-textured soup as the ingredients are chopped rather than blended, which perfectly suits tomato soups and some vegetable soups that I don't want to be silky smooth.

✳ My high-speed, hand-held stick and immersion

blenders produce velvety-smooth soups. I'll use one over the other depending on the amount I'm making (the latter being most suitable for smaller quantities). I also use my high-speed blender for raw soups. I just add the raw ingredients and liquid to the blender and press blend. Mine also has a "soup" function, where the heat of the spinning blades gently heats the liquid so you are left with a warm but technically "raw" soup.

※ You can also use a mouli to purée your soups. This yields a smooth, fine texture.

MAKING, SERVING & STORING TIPS

Now that you've got your base ingredients and blending method sorted out, here are a few tips to help you get the most out of your soup:

※ Always make more than you need. Soups are great to stash away in the freezer for a quick, healthy meal.

※ Save up vegetable trimmings, scraps, or stems and use them to make a full-flavored vegetable stock.

※ Use a good stock (see pages 14–17). The lifeblood of a soup, a well flavored, preferably homemade, vegetable stock will give a great depth of flavor and reduce the need for additional salt or flavorings.

※ Steam-fry your vegetables to reduce the amount of oil needed: sauté them in a small amount of oil; cover with a lid; and let them steam-cook for a few minutes until tender. The natural moisture in the vegetables is normally enough to create a steamy atmosphere in the pan. If not, add a splash of water or stock.

※ Bulk out a soup by adding grated raw vegetables or chopped cooked vegetables just before serving. Also try adding cooked whole grains including brown rice, lentils, barley, quinoa, beans, or chickpeas. These add fiber and give a boost of plant-based protein.

※ Want a dairy-free creamy taste and texture? Add a handful of soaked cashews before blending. Cooked cauliflower, potato, white beans, nondairy yogurt, or a nut-based milk or cream will also work.

※ Need to thicken a soup? Blend in cooked vegetables, such as potatoes, or stir in a handful of rice or oats and simmer until cooked. Adding chunks of stale bread or bread crumbs will absorb some of the liquid. Cornstarch is also an option: mix 1 teaspoon cornstarch with 1 tablespoon cold water until smooth; stir into the soup; simmer, stirring constantly, until thickened.

※ Soup too salty? Starchy food such as potatoes, rice, pasta, or noodles are a great rescue remedy as they absorb some of the salt and their bland flavor helps balance the flavour. A pinch of sugar or the acidity from a little lemon juice or vinegar can help, too.

※ Never let your soup boil. Overheating or overcooking can make vegetables mushy, dull the flavor, and cause nutrient loss. The exceptions are soups that include legumes, or carbs such as pasta.

※ To lift the flavor of a soup, particularly a tomato-based one, add a squeeze of lemon juice or a little finely grated zest at the end of the cooking time.

※ To enrich a soup, add a dollop of cream cheese, milk, or cream. Add a Parmesan rind to a tomato-based soup, or stir in a tablespoon of sherry, brandy, or a lump of butter or nut butter for an instant rich taste.

※ Spices are an easy way to add interest to a soup. I'll often add them when I sauté the vegetables to release their flavor and fragrance. Be careful not to burn them, however, because they can turn bitter.

※ Slow-cookers are perfect for soups that require a long cooking time, such as ones using dried legumes.

※ Soup can improve with keeping. Making it a day ahead can help the flavors meld and develop.

※ Making a large batch of soup with the intention of saving some? Ensure it cools down completely before you store it. Fresh vegetable-based soups normally keep well in an airtight container in the fridge for two to three days and in the freezer for up to one month, after which time the flavors start to degrade. Store soups in freezerproof containers or individually portioned resealable bags for easy defrosting.

※ When it comes to presentation, there are no hard-and-fast rules, but I like to serve my soups in particular vessels because it all adds to the finished look. Thin soups suit daintier bowls or teacups; heartier, chunky soups work in flat, wide bowls or mugs; chilled or sweet soups can be lovely served in glasses, while shot glasses work for palate-cleansing or canapé-style soups.

TOOL KIT

You don't need much in the way of kitchen tools to make soup, other than a cutting board, sharp knife, saucepan, and possibly a blender. For a more extensive tool kit that includes equipment to make toppings and extras, I would include:

* High-speed blender
* Hand-held stick or immersion blender
* Food processor with an "S" blade and different disks for grating
* Microplane graters with different blades for zesting and coarse grating
* Mandoline slicer with various blades
* Selection of sharp knives
* Crinkle cutter knife
* "V" blade channel knives
* Pastry cutters (various shapes)
* Various measuring cups and spoons
* Citrus zester
* Melon ballers (mini and standard-sized)
* Citrus juicer and reamer
* Julienne peeler
* Vegetable peeler
* Leaf stripper
* A spice grinder/coffee bean mill
* Spiralizer
* Stockpot with lid
* Saucepan with lid
* Sauté pan with lid
* Baking pan
* Wooden spoons, spatula, tongs
* Cutting boards

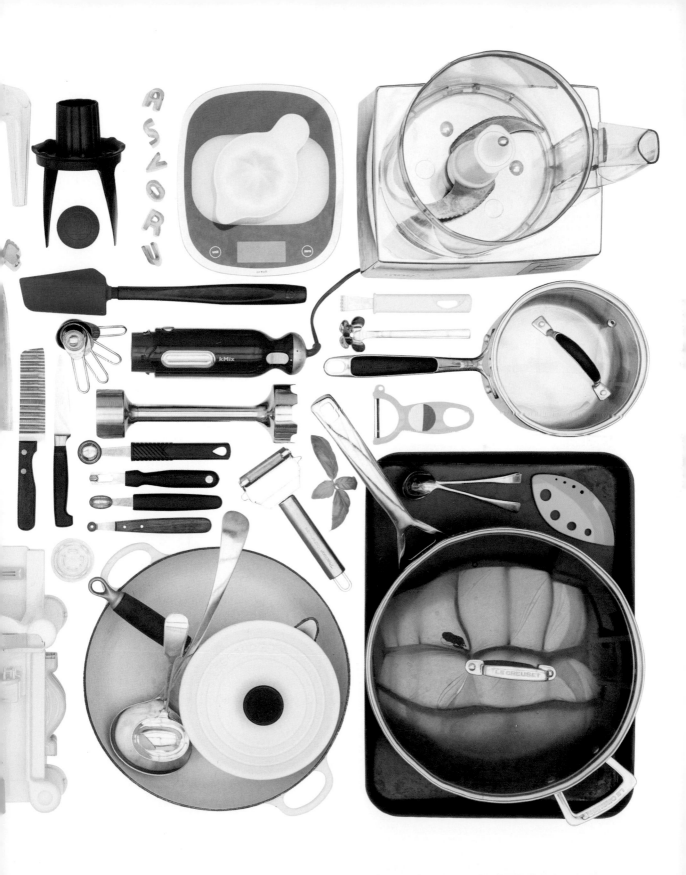

FINISHING TOUCHES

I've already touched on this earlier (see page 8), but a topping can transform an ordinary soup into something special, as well as add additional nutrients, visual interest, texture, and flavor. The following gives you some great ingredients to dollop, drizzle, spoon, sprinkle, or scatter on top of your soups (also see Toppings & Sprinkles pages 128–139):

✳ OILS: good extra virgin olive oil, avocado oil, herb oil, and flavored oil, including lemon, chile, and sesame oil.

✳ VINEGARS: balsamic and white balsamic vinegar.

✳ SAUCES: homemade Sriracha (see page 135), soy sauce, teriyaki sauce, Worcestershire sauce, aïoli, harissa, red and green Thai curry paste, pesto, salsa, mustard, tahini.

✳ YOGURT & CREAM: Greek yogurt, goat-milk yogurt, Raw Almond Yogurt (see page 137), Raw Cashew Cream (see page 138), sour cream, raita, labneh.

✳ PROTEIN: marinated tofu or tempeh, shredded meat, such as cooked chicken, pork, or beef, crumbled crispy bacon, frazzled chorizo, mini meatballs.

✳ CHEESE: grated hard cheese, diced paneer, marinated feta, diced fresh mozzarella or burrata, Parmesan chips.

✳ EGGS: poached or fried eggs, hard-boiled quail eggs, ribbons of pancake or omelet, bite-sized pieces of frittata.

✳ FISH: flaked salmon or smoked mackerel, slivers of smoked salmon, cooked brown shrimp, mini fishcakes, flaked crabmeat.

✳ RAW VEGETABLES: finely shredded greens, such as spinach, Swiss chard, or cabbage, grated or spiralized zucchini, carrot, beet, or sweet potato, Raw Vegetable Confetti (see page 31), shaved truffles, peas, corn, finely sliced fennel or asparagus, shaved parsnips, shredded leeks, "riced" zucchini or cauliflower.

✳ RAW FRUIT: pomegranate seeds, finely diced avocado or tomato, finely sliced fresh chile, citrus zest, apple matchsticks, frozen mixed berries.

✳ DRIED VEGETABLES: dehydrated vegetable chips or powders (see page 131), seaweed confetti or spaghetti.

✳ PRESERVED & CURED: olives, capers, juniper berries, kimchi, sauerkraut, sun-dried tomatoes, pickled peppers.

✳ COOKED TOPPINGS: gnocchi, dumplings, gyoza, wontons, gougères, Matzo Balls (see page 101), falafel.

✳ NUTS & SEEDS: whole, crushed, or toasted nuts and seeds; sweet or Savory Granola (see page 131); poppy seeds, hemp seeds, sunflower seeds, sesame seeds, pine nuts, flaked almonds, crushed dry-roast peanuts.

✳ CROUTONS: sourdough, rye bread, potato, sweet potato, polenta, cheese-topped toast.

✳ SUPERFOODS: spirulina powder, bee pollen, flaxseeds, goji berries.

✳ CHIPS: homemade root vegetable or tortilla chips.

✳ COOKED GRAINS/SEEDS/LEGUMES: faro, freekeh, buckwheat, quinoa, amaranth, couscous, brown rice, lentils, beans, barley, chickpeas.

✳ COOKED VEGETABLES: roast vegetables, sweet potato wedges, Cauliflower Steaks (see page 134), caramelized or crispy onions; steamed vegetables, such as sugar snap peas, green beans, and broccoli florets; kale chips, crispy vegetable tempura, mini rösti, and Crispy Sprout Leaves (see page 132).

✳ SPROUTING SEEDS: pea shoots, sunflower sprouts, mixed sprouting seeds.

✳ SPICES: sumac, saffron, paprika, and dried chile flakes; spice mixes, such as Za'atar, Panch Phoran, and Dukkah (see page 128), garam masala and ras-el-hanout; whole spices, including mustard seeds, pink peppercorns, caraway, fennel, cumin, nigella, and juniper.

✳ HERBS: fresh herbs, including mint, basil, parsley, dill, thyme, and chives, dried herbs, and dried herb powders.

✳ EDIBLE FLOWERS: fresh roses, primroses, violets, fuchsias, marigolds, borage, and ramson flowers, dried flowers, including rose petals, calendula, and hibiscus.

✳ DRIED FRUIT: cranberries, barberries, freeze-dried raspberries and strawberries, sun-dried tomatoes.

WHAT MAKES A GOOD STOCK?

A good stock can truly be liquid gold in the kitchen. Just one ladleful has the ability to transform—and infuse flavor and fragrance into—many dishes, including stews, sauces, and risottos.

A great-tasting stock doesn't have to be made out of bones to have depth of flavor and richness. A vegetable-based stock can be equally tasty, even if the layers of flavors are a little less complex.

Vegetable stock can be exceptionally nutritious and drinkable. Just add a few rice noodles, some wilted greens, or finely grated raw vegetables and you have a comforting, restorative, and rejuvenating meal in minutes.

I usually make vegetable stocks in four different ways: a cooked stock; a quick light stock; a raw stock; and a dehydrated vegetable powder stock. Recipes for all are included on the following pages.

TIPS FOR MAKING COOKED VEGETABLE STOCK:

✳ It sounds obvious but always start with the freshest (preferably organic) ingredients. Use big-flavored fruit and vegetables and a selection of herbs and spices.

✳ To retain as many nutrients and flavors as possible, don't boil your stock. Start with cold water and slowly bring to a simmer.

✳ Cut the vegetables into small pieces, rather than large chunks. This reduces cooking time and helps to extract the flavors as well as preserving the vitamins and minerals.

✳ For a richer flavor and deeper color, lightly sauté the onion, carrot, and celery in a little oil until browned before you add them to the stock pot.

✳ Keep any leftover herb stems to use in stocks because these are loaded with flavor.

✳ If you want a clear stock, don't use starchy vegetables like potatoes. These can thicken the stock and make it cloudy.

✳ Unless you're making the stock for a specific recipe, omit strongly flavored ingredients, such as garlic, fennel, seaweed, whole spices, lemon grass, ginger, or chiles. These can unbalance the flavor of the stock and then overpower a more delicate-tasting soup.

✳ Some ingredients can act as subtle flavor enhancers without being too strong. Mushrooms give a lovely, rich umami taste, whereas a bouquet garni (a bundle of different herbs tied together) made with parsley, thyme, bay leaves, rosemary, and/or marjoram will provide a wonderful herbal infusion and fragrance.

✳ To keep the stock clear and fresh-tasting, skim off any "scum" or froth that rises to the surface using a spoon or a strainer with a fine wire mesh.

✳ Strain your stock when ready using a chinois, a cheesecloth-lined sieve, or a nut-milk bag.

✳ Store the stock in an airtight container in the fridge or freezer. If freezing, let the stock cool completely before pouring into smaller containers or an ice-cube tray (this makes for quick and easy defrosting).

COOKED VEGETABLE STOCK

This is my highly customizable basic stock recipe. If I'm making it for a specific soup, I tend to keep to the three magic ingredients of carrot, onion, and celery and then choose the other ingredients to suit the flavor of the soup I'm making.

4 small carrots, cut into medium dice

3 celery stalks, cut into medium dice

2 large onions or 2 medium leeks, cut in half

1 bay leaf

1 small bunch of mixed herbs, such as parsley, thyme, and rosemary

2 teaspoon black peppercorns

2 quarts water

Place the carrots, celery, and onions in a large saucepan with the bay leaf, herbs, and peppercorns. Add the measured water. It should cover the vegetables completely by 2 to 3¼ inches; you might need to add more depending on the size of your pan.

Bring to a gentle simmer and cook for 40 to 50 minutes, occasionally skimming off any froth that rises to the surface, until the stock tastes rich and full. Take care not to overcook the vegetables or the flavor will become stale and flat.

Strain the stock, discarding the solids. Use immediately or store in an airtight container in the fridge for up to 1 week, or freeze for 1 to 2 months.

QUICK "NO-RECIPE" LIGHT VEGETABLE STOCK

This handy broth can be used as a base for soups, sauces, or stews, or just enjoyed on its own as a restorative elixir. It's a simple, no-recipe formula that's easy to prepare and can be frozen in ice-cube trays for quick defrosting.

It's an excellent way to use up any odds and ends, vegetable scraps, or vegetables wilting in the crisper. Because this broth is only cooked briefly it's fine to add strongly flavored vegetables like cabbage or broccoli, which you would normally avoid in a stock. For a quick, filling meal, add other types of vegetables, cooked protein, and carbs.

3 large handfuls of mixed vegetables, such as carrots, celery, onions, leeks, cauliflower, cabbage, and broccoli, cut into small pieces

1 small handful of herbs, such as thyme, parsley, and rosemary

1 small handful of other flavorings, such as 6 to 7 black peppercorns, 1 to 2 bay leaves, 1 large garlic clove, 1 small dried chile, 1 small piece fresh ginger root, or a few dried mushrooms

salt and pepper

Place the vegetables in a large saucepan with the herbs and your choice of flavorings, such as bay leaves and peppercorns.

Cover with water and bring to a boil, then turn the heat down and let simmer for 15 to 20 minutes until the vegetables are tender but not overcooked.

Strain the liquid (discarding the herbs, flavorings, and vegetables), season to taste with salt and pepper, and either use immediately or let cool.

Cover and store in an airtight container in the fridge for 3 to 5 days, or store in the freezer for 1 to 3 months.

RAW VEGETABLE STOCK

My raw vegetable stock adds a flavor boost to raw soups and salad dressings and, if I'm feeling run down, I like to drink a straight shot of it as an elixir. I make it by juicing a variety of fruits, vegetables, herbs, and spices to create a rich, intense juice with a mixture of super-concentrated flavorings.

As with the Cooked Vegetable Stock (see page 15), this raw alternative can be treated as a foundation recipe to which you add other ingredients depending on how you're going to use it. For instance, if I'm using it as a stock for a spicy Asian-style soup, I might add a thumb-sized piece of fresh turmeric, a handful of fresh cilantro, ¼ teaspoon cumin seeds, and a stalk of lemon grass. Fennel also gives it an aniseedy kick. Unlike the cooked vegetable stock, however, I rarely add carrots because they can be very sweet, and I prefer to keep the flavors clean and savory.

⅓ red onion, peeled, or ½ large leek, trimmed

2 to 3 garlic cloves, peeled and left whole

¾- to 1¼-inch piece fresh ginger root, peeled

4 celery stalks

1 jalapeño chile or red or green chile, seeded if you prefer less heat

1 small bunch of mixed herbs, such as parsley, basil, cilantro, dill, rosemary, and marjoram

sea salt flakes

Run all the ingredients through a slow juicer. Pour the liquid into a large pitcher or bowl, stir, and season to taste with salt, if desired. Alternatively, you can add extra juiced celery, since it is naturally high in salt. Store in an airtight container in the fridge for 1 to 2 days.

DEHYDRATED VEGETABLE STOCK POWDER

It's always handy to have a pot of instant vegetable stock powder as part of your kitchen cupboard essentials but store-bought varieties can taste a little musty or overly salty. However, by making your own you know exactly what's in it. The vegetables all need to be washed, dried, and very thinly sliced before they are dehydrated; a mandoline slicer is the perfect tool for slicing them.

4 large carrots, very thinly sliced

2 large red onions, very thinly sliced

2 large zucchini, very thinly sliced

2 red bell peppers, seeded and very thinly sliced

3 to 4 large mushrooms, very thinly sliced

3 to 4 celery stalks, very thinly sliced

4 large tomatoes, very thinly sliced

4 garlic cloves, very thinly sliced

1 small handful of mixed herb leaves, such as parsley, dill, cilantro, and oregano

1 teaspoon ground paprika

1 teaspoon kelp powder

2 teaspoon sea salt flakes, or to taste

pepper

Preheat the oven to 150°F or set it as low as it will go. Or, use a dehydrator and follow the manufacturer's instructions.

Arrange the prepared vegetables and herbs in a single layer on wire racks set inside or on top of baking pans or cookie sheets.

Place in the oven for 3 to 5 hours, turning once, or until completely dry and brittle; you may need to do this in batches. Remove from the oven and let cool completely.

Using a high-speed blender, coffee mill, or spice grinder, blitz the dehydrated ingredients in batches to a fine powder. Tip the powder into a large bowl, then stir in the paprika, kelp powder, salt, and pepper to combine. Season to taste with extra salt and pepper, if needed.

To use, stir the stock powder directly into warm liquids, sauces, and stews or add 2 teaspoons stock powder to a heatproof bowl along with 1¼ cups boiling water, then stir to combine. Taste and add more stock powder, if needed.

Store the powder in an airtight container in a cool place for up to 2 months.

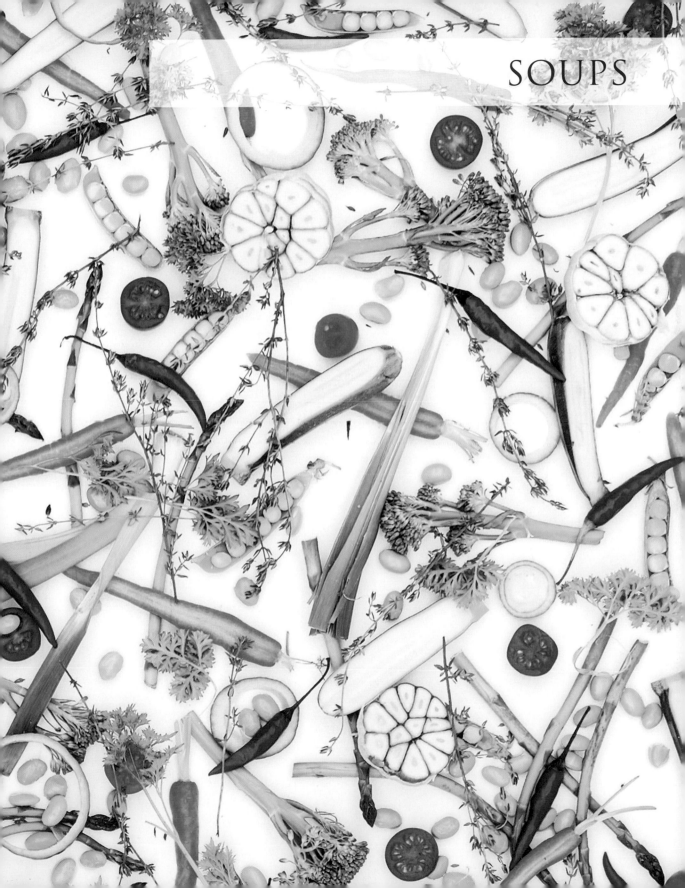

CURRIED GREENS & COCONUT SOUP

This mixed-greens soup is mildly hot and delicately perfumed with spices.
I first ate a version of this at a beachside cooking class while on vacation in the
Maldives. The base of the soup can be made in advance and the cooked green
vegetables added at the last minute.

SERVES 2 TO 3

2 tablespoons olive oil ❊ 1 large onion, finely chopped

2-inch piece fresh ginger root, peeled and finely chopped

3 garlic cloves, finely chopped ❊ ¾ oz curry leaves

2 cinnamon sticks, broken in half if large ❊ 5 cardamom pods, bruised

5 whole cloves ❊ ½ teaspoon garam masala ❊ ½ teaspoon ground turmeric

¼ teaspoon ground cumin ❊ 1 tablespoon tomato paste

1 cup coconut cream ❊ 1 cup hot Cooked Vegetable Stock (see page 15)

1lb 10 oz mixed greens (broccoli florets, green beans, bok choy, zucchini, asparagus, Swiss
chard, spinach, fennel, whatever you have on hand), coarsely chopped or thinly sliced

salt and pepper

TO SERVE

¼ cup chopped cilantro leaves

2 to 3 tablespoons freshly grated or shaved coconut ❊ 2 limes, cut into wedges

Heat the oil in a large sauté pan, add the onion, and fry gently until translucent.

Add the ginger, garlic, curry leaves, and spices and cook, stirring constantly, for a few
minutes until they release their fragrance. Stir in the tomato paste, coconut cream, and stock
then simmer for 5 minutes or until thickened. Season to taste with salt and pepper.

Gently steam (or sauté) the greens, or keep them raw if preferred.
Divide the greens among serving bowls, saving some to garnish.

To serve, ladle the soup onto the greens. Top each serving with the reserved greens,
the cilantro, and coconut, with wedges of lime on the side.

Nutrition tip

Top off your levels of folic acid, vitamin C, and antioxidants with this green soup.
The coconut milk supplies MCTs (medium chain triglycerides),
which can help improve fat-to-muscle ratios in the body.

TRY ADDING shrimp, fresh tuna, or shredded chicken for a protein boost.

VELVETY BEET SOUP

This smooth, vibrant soup is great for your health thanks to the beet—an amazing nutritional powerhouse. The crisp Paneer Bites (see page 134) and Popped Pumpkin Seeds (see page 130) give a crunchy contrast to the velvety-textured soup.

SERVES 2 TO 3

6 large raw beets, scrubbed, stems and leaves removed

1¾ cups hot Cooked Vegetable Stock (see page 15) ❋ juice of ½ lemon

¼ cup Raw Almond Yogurt (see page 137) or yogurt of your choice

salt and pepper

TO SERVE

½ teaspoon grated fresh horseradish

3 tablespoons Raw Sour Cashew Cream (see page 138)

Marinated "Paneer Bites" (see page 134) ❋ Popped Pumpkin Seeds (see page 130)

dill sprigs, to garnish

Place the beets in a large saucepan, cover with cold water, and bring to a boil. Cook the beets, covered, at a robust simmer for 50 to 60 minutes until tender, then drain and let cool.

When cool enough to handle, remove the skins—they should slip off quite easily but wear rubber gloves to stop the juice from staining your fingers. Chop the beet into large chunks.

Add the beet to a food processor with the other ingredients and blitz to a silky smooth consistency. You could use a hand-held stick blender, but beware the potentially permanent purple splatters! Season to taste with salt and pepper, and refrigerate for 2 to 3 hours if serving chilled.

Before serving, mix the horseradish with the sour cream.

To serve, ladle the soup into bowls and scatter with the paneer bites and pumpkin seeds. Drizzle with the horseradish cream and then garnish with a sprig of dill before enjoying warm or chilled.

Nutrition tip

This soup really maxes out on beet benefits. Perhaps tuck into a bowl or two before a run if you want to try improving your time!

❋

SAVE THE BEET STEMS AND LEAVES—they are a great source of nutrition. Beet leaves contain more iron than spinach. Juice and drink the stems and use the raw leaves in a salad or finely chopped to garnish the soup.

MISO BROTHS

Miso soup is so easy to make and I love serving it with a buffet of "fixin's" to allow everyone to add their own choice of toppings, flavorings, and sprinkles. The added extras can provide a contrast of taste, texture, and color, so it's good to offer a few different options, including crunchy vegetables, soft noodles, or spicy fresh ginger.

SERVES 3 TO 4

3½ cups Vegan Dashi (see page 138)

1 tablespoon dried seaweed, such as nori or wakame

2 tablespoons miso paste (white or dark, or a mixture of both)

2 to 3 scallions, finely sliced ❄ 1 to 2 teaspoons sesame oil

salt and pepper

TO SERVE

a selection of fixin's, including finely sliced radishes, spiralized carrots or zucchini, cucumber noodles or ribbons, celery leaves, finely sliced leeks, mushrooms or chiles, edamame beans, finely grated fresh ginger root, cooked glass or soba noodles, and sliced bok choy

Pour the dashi into a large saucepan and bring almost to a boil. Add the seaweed and simmer for 2 minutes.

Put the miso paste in a small bowl, add 2 tablespoons of the dashi broth, and beat until dissolved. Then pour it back into the pan. Add the scallions and simmer briefly. Season to taste with salt and pepper.

To serve, pour into individual glass cups or bowls, top with the fixin's of your choice, and drizzle with sesame oil.

Nutrition tip

Miso paste is a fermented food that can help the good bacteria in your gut thrive. These good bacteria help keep your digestive and immune systems healthy.

ADD cubes of tofu for added protein.

STIR IN cooked wild or brown rice for a more substantial meal.

SERVE AS a Japanese vegetable stew—simmer the fixin's in the soup instead of separately.

CREAMY CHICKPEA SOUP

The mild flavor of the chickpeas is spiced with sumac, while the capers give a nice briny tang. Chickpeas are high in protein and become rich, creamy, and comforting when they're blended.

SERVES 3 TO 4

1 cup dried chickpeas ✳ 1 tablespoon olive oil or coconut oil

1 onion, finely chopped ✳ 1 carrot, finely chopped

2 celery stalks, finely chopped ✳ 1 to 2 garlic cloves, finely chopped

1 teaspoon sumac, plus extra for sprinkling

1½ cups hot Cooked Vegetable Stock (see page 15)

1 to 2 tablespoons preserved capers, rinsed and drained, plus extra to garnish

salt and pepper

Put the chickpeas in a bowl and cover with plenty of cold water. Let soak overnight and then drain.

Place the chickpeas in a large saucepan and cover with fresh cold water. Bring to a boil, then turn the heat down and let simmer for about 1 hour, or until tender. Drain the chickpeas and set aside until ready to use.

Heat the oil in a large saucepan, add the onion, carrot, celery, garlic, and sumac and fry gently until the vegetables have softened. Add the cooked chickpeas (reserve a few to garnish) and stock, and let simmer for a few minutes to heat through. Stir in the capers.

Remove the pan from the heat and blend until smooth and creamy using a hand-held stick blender, or blend in a food processor, adding a little extra stock if the soup is too thick. Season to taste with salt and pepper, bearing in mind that the capers are quite salty.

To serve, ladle the soup into bowls and scatter with the reserved chickpeas and a few extra capers, then sprinkle with a little sumac.

Nutrition tip

You'll get a good boost of fiber from this soup, courtesy of the chickpeas, and much of this kind of fiber is the soluble type that can help reduce cholesterol.

STIR IN a handful of baby spinach at the same time as the chickpeas to add a fresh green element. You could also serve the soup unblended.

SPRINKLE with a handful of grated Parmesan cheese or nutritional yeast flakes just before serving.

FOR A CURRIED CHICKPEA SOUP, omit the capers and add your favorite curry powder, to taste. Also, try replacing the stock with coconut milk to give a lovely creamy texture and flavor, as well as complement the curry spices.

SUPER-GREENS SOUP

This very "green" soup is high in plant protein from the kale, spinach, and broccoli. It's also extremely alkaline and only lightly cooked so easier on the digestive system. A sprinkling of bee pollen and spirulina powder gives an extra superfood boost, and dehydrated herb or vegetable powder enhances the flavor.

SERVES 3 TO 4

2 leeks, very finely chopped ✳ 2 celery stalks, finely chopped

½ head of broccoli, cut into small florets

3 to 4 large kale leaves, about 5½ to 7oz total weight,
tough stalks removed, and leaves torn into large pieces

4 to 6 asparagus spears, woody ends broken off, sliced into 1-inch pieces

1 small handful of parsley, leaves only ✳ 1 small handful of mint, leaves only

3½ cups hot Cooked Vegetable Stock (see page 15)

salt and pepper

TO SERVE

1 tablespoon bee pollen ✳ 1 teaspoon spirulina powder

1 teaspoon Dehydrated Herb or Vegetable Powder (see page 131)

Using a multi-tier steamer, layer the vegetables starting with the ones that take the longest to cook closest to the water. So, from the bottom up, start with leeks, then celery, broccoli, kale, and finally the asparagus. Lightly steam the vegetables for 10 to 15 minutes until just cooked.

If you don't have a steamer, lightly cook the vegetables in simmering water until just tender.

Add the vegetables to a high-speed blender or a food processor, add the parsley, mint, and stock and blitz to a smooth consistency. Season to taste with salt and pepper.

To serve, ladle the soup into bowls and sprinkle with the bee pollen, spirulina, and dehydrated herb or vegetable powder.

Nutrition tip

Crammed full of folic acid, as well as cell-protective antioxidants,
this really does live up to it's "super" label healthwise.

FOR A MORE SUBSTANTIAL MEAL, add cooked potatoes, beans, lentils, or quinoa.

SCATTER with a handful of protein-rich toasted nuts or seeds for added crunch.

SQUEEZE IN the juice of a lemon or grapefruit to add a citrus tang; the vitamin C from the citrus fruit will also aid the absorption of iron from the green vegetables.

SERVE the soup chilled instead of warm.

CONFETTI SOUP

You can make this soup using any clear soup, consommé, or light vegetable broth. Try my Quick "No-Recipe" Light Vegetable Stock (see page 16), or just a good store-bought vegetable bouillon powder or cube. The trick is that you should be able to see the "confetti" in the soup, all the way down to the ones that might have sunk to the bottom of the bowl.

SERVES 2 TO 3

2 to 3 baby zucchini ❋ 3 to 4 baby corn on the cob, thinly sliced crosswise

3 to 4 large radishes, cut into thin matchsticks

1 small root vegetable, such as a carrot, beet, or parsnip, cut into small dice

3 cups Quick "No-Recipe" Light Vegetable Stock (see page 16)
or vegetable bouillon, or clear soup

1 small handful of peas or sugar snap peas

1 small handful of delicate herbs, such as fennel, basil, dill, and chives,
finely chopped, plus extra to garnish

1 small handful of pomegranate seeds ❋ salt and pepper

Score the skin of the baby zucchini lengthwise to make shallow, v-shaped grooves then slice very thinly crossways. Gently mix the zucchini with the baby corn, radishes, and diced root vegetable of choice.

Gently heat the vegetable stock and stir in the confetti vegetable shapes, peas or sugar snaps, herbs, and pomegranate seeds. Simmer for a few minutes to warm everything through then season to taste with salt and pepper.

To serve, ladle the broth into bowls and scatter with a few extra herbs

Nutrition tip

Despite being light on calories, this soup will fill you up and has a good content of potassium, which helps to maintain a healthy blood pressure.

YOU CAN MAKE "confetti" out of any raw vegetables as long as you cut or slice them finely enough. Very finely diced rainbow chard stems make beautiful multicolored sprinkles; shaved broccoli florets turn into tiny broccoli grains (this works well with purple-sprouting broccoli, cauliflower, and bright green Romanesco, too); thinly sliced pink or purple radicchio form vibrant ribbons; or try scattering the soup with a selection of tiny edible leaves and flowers.

FRESH TOMATO SOUP

This is almost like a fresh savory smoothie and is completely raw. You can, of course, gently warm the soup—just don't heat it too much or cook it for too long, otherwise the soup loses its freshness and the tomatoes become watery.

SERVES 2 TO 3

4 to 6 large ripe tomatoes, coarsely chopped

2 red bell peppers, seeded and coarsely chopped

1 to 2 celery stalks, coarsely chopped ❋ ½ onion, coarsely chopped

½ red chile pepper, seeded and coarsely chopped

½ small garlic clove, coarsely chopped

1 small handful of parsley, coarsely chopped

½ cup Raw Vegetable Stock (see page 16) or water

1 small handful of basil leaves ❋ salt and pepper

Add the tomatoes, red bell peppers, celery, onion, chile, garlic, parsley, and stock or water to a high-speed blender or food processor. Blitz to a finely chopped, soupy consistency. Add more water, or blend for longer, if you prefer a thinner soup. Season to taste with salt and pepper.

To serve, ladle the soup into bowls, or serve in chilled glasses, with a few basil leaves to garnish.

Nutrition tip

Even very small amounts of parsley provide good amounts of vitamin K, which is important for normal blood clotting and strong bones.

BLEND in a handful of soaked cashews or the flesh of ½ avocado for a creamy soup. Serve as a dip with crudités.

BLEND for slightly longer to make a very smooth soup then serve as a salad dressing, or as a sauce for a raw main meal with spiralized zucchini or cucumber noodles.

ADD a dash of Tabasco or Worcestershire sauce and use as a base for a Bloody Mary.

SWISS CHARD & CELERY SOUP

Celery and the stems of Swiss chard are naturally high in sodium so you may find that you hardly need to add any salt to this soup.

SERVES 3 TO 4

2 tablespoons olive oil or coconut oil ❊ 1 red onion, finely chopped

4 to 5 celery stalks, finely chopped, leaves reserved

3 to 4 garlic cloves, peeled and left whole

1 large bunch of Swiss chard, stems finely chopped and leaves torn into large pieces

1 small rosemary sprig, needles finely chopped

1 small bunch of parsley, leaves only

2½ cups hot Cooked Vegetable Stock (see page 15) ❊ salt and pepper

Heat the oil in a large saucepan, add the onion, celery, garlic, chard stems, and rosemary and fry gently until the vegetables have softened.

Stir in the chard leaves, parsley, and stock and let simmer for 5 to 10 minutes until the chard leaves are tender.

Remove the pan from the heat and blend the soup to a rough purée using a hand-held stick blender, or blend in a food processor. Season to taste with salt and pepper.

To serve, ladle the soup into bowls and scatter with a few celery leaves to garnish.

Nutrition tip

Nutritious and hydrating, this is a slimline soup. Swiss chard is a source of anemia-protective iron and the antioxidant vitamin E.

CRUMBLED crispy bacon adds an extra savory flavor.

STIR IN a handful of cooked beans, such as cannellini, navy, or lima beans for a more filling dish with added fiber.

ADD A DOLLOP of a spicy tomato salsa or red bell pepper pesto.

SOUPY SALAD

The soup part is simply juiced vegetables, which you can gently warm up if you prefer, while the salad part is similar to coleslaw, made with shredded and grated raw vegetables. The salad adds texture and body to the soup, as do a few chopped or ground nuts and seeds. It might not sound promising as a dish, but I assure you it's really tasty and leaves you feeling full, yet still light.

SERVES 3 TO 4
FOR THE SOUP

3 to 4 large carrots, chopped into chunks ❉ 4 large tomatoes, chopped into large chunks

2 to 3 celery stalks, chopped into chunks

1 lemon grass stalk, outer layer discarded, chopped into small pieces

1 small handful of basil leaves ❉ 1 garlic clove, peeled, and left whole

salt and pepper ❉ mixed nuts and seeds, chopped, to serve (optional)

FOR THE SALAD

2 large carrots, coarsely grated ❉ 2 celery stalks, finely chopped, leaves reserved to garnish

2 small Little Gem lettuces, finely shredded ❉ 1 raw beet, scrubbed and coarsely grated

1 small bunch of parsley, finely chopped

To make the soup, run all the ingredients through a juicer. Season to taste with salt and pepper and chill in the fridge for 2 to 3 hours, or until ready to serve.

For the salad, mix together all the ingredients.

To serve, place a large spoonful of the salad into each serving bowl, then add some soup. Scatter with the chopped nuts and seeds, if desired, and add a few chopped celery leaves.

Nutrition tip

There's a lot of beta-carotene in this soup, which can be turned into vitamin A. It's great for keeping your immune system healthy.

JUICE any savory-flavored fruits or vegetables to make the soup and add a pinch of ground spices, if you want to turn up the heat.

MAKE the salad part using any finely shredded or chopped raw fruits or vegetables, and add a little chopped dried fruit for a chewy sweetness.

SWAP things around and serve the salad with some of the soup spooned over as a dressing.

LOOKING to break the monotony of a juice cleanse? This is a great soup to turn to.

SWEET POTATO & PEAR SOUP

This delicate soup can be served warm or chilled, but for a more intense, robust flavor, roast the sweet potatoes and pears before blending.

SERVES 4 TO 6

2 tablespoons vegan butter ❋ 1 onion, finely chopped

3 large sweet potatoes, peeled and cut into small chunks

2 to 3 large ripe pears, cut into large chunks,
plus extra, finely chopped, to garnish

2½ cups hot Quick "No-Recipe" Light Vegetable Stock (see page 16)

¼ cup Macadamia Cream Cheese (see page 137) or any dairy or vegan cream cheese alternative

salt and pepper

Melt the butter in a large saucepan, add the onion, and fry gently until softened. Add the sweet potatoes and pears and sauté for a few minutes.

Add the stock and simmer for 15 to 20 minutes until the sweet potatoes are tender, then stir in the cream cheese.

Remove the pan from the heat and blend until smooth using a hand-held stick blender, or blend in a food processor. Season to taste with salt and pepper

To serve, ladle the soup into teacups or small bowls and scatter with a little chopped pear.

Nutrition tip

Sweet potatoes have a healthily low GI, so eating them will help keep your blood-sugar level steady. In addition, they're a good source of vitamin A, which is important for the immune system.

CRUMBLE a little blue cheese or goat cheese on the top—the flavors go together beautifully.

SCATTER with a few toasted flaked almonds, or shards of crispy pancetta or smoky bacon for added crunch.

GARNISH with a few edible flowers for a pretty finishing touch.

IF SERVING CHILLED, a little splash of eau de vie, such as Poire William, gives a nice boozy finish.

CHUNKY CRANBERRY BEAN & KALE SOUP

I've used cooked dried cranberry beans in this chunky soup, but you could use canned instead to save time. Cavolo nero or Savoy cabbage could also be used instead of the kale in this rustic, Italian-style soup.

SERVES 3 TO 4

1½ cups dried cranberry beans, rinsed and drained

2 tablespoons olive oil or coconut oil ✳ 1 red onion, finely chopped

1 carrot, finely chopped ✳ 1 celery stalk, finely chopped

2 to 3 garlic cloves, finely chopped

2 small red chiles, seeded and finely chopped, plus extra to garnish

1 teaspoon fennel seeds ✳ 4 to 6 large ripe tomatoes, coarsely chopped

4 to 5 kale leaves, stems removed and leaves chopped into large pieces

1 small handful of parsley leaves, coarsely chopped

2 cups hot Cooked Vegetable Stock (see page 15) ✳ salt and pepper

Put the beans in a bowl and cover with plenty of cold water. Let soak overnight, and then drain.

Place the beans in a large saucepan and cover with fresh cold water. Bring to a boil, then turn the heat down and let simmer for about 1 hour, or until tender. Drain the beans and set aside until ready to use.

Heat the oil in a large saucepan, add the onion, carrot, celery, garlic, chile, and fennel seeds and cook gently until the vegetables have softened.

Add the cooked beans, tomatoes, kale (reserve a little to garnish), parsley, and stock and let simmer for 10 to 15 minutes until the vegetables are cooked and the tomatoes tender.

Remove the pan from the heat and part-blend the soup using a hand-held stick blender, or blend in a food processor if you want a thick, creamy consistency. Or, leave the soup unblended for a more rustic, chunky texture. Season to taste with salt and pepper.

To serve, ladle the soup into bowls. Scatter with a little chopped red chile and the reserved kale.

Nutrition tip

Kale provides lutein, an antioxidant believed to be good for protecting your eyes.

SERVE with crusty rustic bread, or stir in a handful of cooked pasta for a more substantial minestrone-style soup.

ADD spicy cured sausage or salami, crispy pancetta, or cooked ham.

A HANDFUL of grated Parmesan cheese and a few torn basil leaves complement the flavors of the soup.

BROCCOLI & LEMON SOUP

Making this soup is a great way of using the whole broccoli, stalk and all. The lemon balances the slightly sulfurous taste that cooked broccoli can sometimes have, while the sriracha sauce gives the soup a sweet-spicy finish.

SERVES 3 TO 4

1 to 2 tablespoons olive oil ❋ 1 onion, finely chopped

1 to 2 garlic cloves, finely chopped ❋ 2 to 3 celery stalks, coarsely chopped

1 head of broccoli, broken into small florets, stalk reserved

2½ cups hot Cooked Vegetable Stock (see page 15)

juice and finely grated zest of 1 lemon, plus extra lemon slices to garnish

1 small red chile, seeded and finely chopped

1 small handful of basil leaves ❋ salt and pepper

Sriracha Sauce (see page 135), to serve

Heat half of the oil in a large saucepan, add the onion, garlic, and celery and fry gently until softened but not colored.

Add the broccoli florets and stock and simmer for 10 to 15 minutes until the broccoli is tender. Add the lemon juice and zest.

While the soup is cooking, peel the broccoli stalk and slice it very finely crosswise (a mandoline slicer is ideal for this). Toss the sliced broccoli stalk with the chile and salt and pepper and dress with the remaining olive oil.

The soup should now be ready. Remove the pan from the heat and blend the soup to a silky-smooth consistency using a hand-held stick blender, or blend in a food processor. Season to taste with salt and pepper.

To serve, ladle the soup into bowls and scatter each serving with the sliced broccoli stalks and basil leaves. Top with lemon slices and drizzle with sriracha.

Nutrition tip

Broccoli is a really good source of folic acid, essential for making red blood cells. The vitamin is also essential prior to, and in the early stages of, pregnancy.

CRUMBLE goat cheese, ricotta, or blue cheese onto the soup.

TRY fresh mint instead of lemon as a flavoring.

THIS SOUP is also lovely chilled with maybe a little diced cucumber mixed in to give freshness and texture.

USE lemon oil instead of olive oil to dress the broccoli-stalk garnish.

PUMPKIN SOUP

Pumpkin, like other kinds of squash, is delicious roasted because it becomes sweet and rich. The curry spices complement the pumpkin and give an extra warming flavor. Keep the seeds from the pumpkin, clean to remove any fibers, then roast and scatter onto the soup before serving.

SERVES 3 TO 4

1 medium pumpkin, cut in half, seeded (keep the seeds for roasting), peeled, and cut into large chunks

1 large onion, coarsely chopped ❋ 2 to 3 tablespoons olive oil or melted coconut oil

2 teaspoons garam masala ❋ 3½ cups hot Cooked Vegetable Stock (see page 15)

salt and pepper

TO SERVE

2 to 3 tablespoons Raw Cashew Cream (see page 138)

2 to 3 tablespoons Popped Savory Quinoa (see page 130)

2 to 3 tablespoons Roasted Pumpkin Seeds (see page 130)

Preheat the oven to 375°F.

Mix the pumpkin and onion with the oil and garam masala in a large bowl to coat, then add to a large roasting pan. Spread the vegetables out in an even layer and roast for 30 to 40 minutes until the pumpkin is golden and cooked through.

Add the roasted pumpkin and onion to a food processor with the stock and blend until silky smooth. Season to taste with salt and pepper.

To serve, ladle the soup into mugs or bowls and serve topped with a swirl of cashew cream. Sprinkle with the popped quinoa and scatter with the roasted pumpkin seeds.

Nutrition tip

The orange color of pumpkin signifies that it's a great source of carotenoids, a type of antioxidant that helps protect cells against damaging free radicals.

SERVE SPRINKLED with nutritional yeast flakes or grated cheese, and chunks of rustic bread for dunking.
POUR INTO a hollowed-out pumpkin or squash shell for a fun way to serve the soup at a Halloween party.
ADD coconut milk or coconut cream for an extra rich, creamy finish, or blend in a couple of tablespoons of almond butter or peanut butter for added protein.

LEEK & POTATO SOUP

Vichyssoise is a classic soup that's lovely served warm or chilled. Use a firm-fleshed, waxy round white or round red variety of potato, such as Yukon Gold or Norland to give a good flavor and creamy texture.

SERVES 3 TO 4

2 to 3 large waxy potatoes, scrubbed and finely diced ✳ 2 to 3 tablespoons vegan butter

3 to 4 large leeks, coarsely chopped, plus extra finely sliced to garnish

1 large onion, finely chopped ✳ 1¾ cups hot Cooked Vegetable Stock (see page 15)

pinch of freshly grated nutmeg

½ cup Raw Cashew Cream (see page 138) or any dairy or vegan cream alternative

salt and pepper ✳ favorite crackers, to serve

Cook the potatoes in a saucepan of boiling salted water until tender, then drain.

While the potatoes are cooking, heat the butter in a separate large pan, add the leeks and onion, and sauté gently for 3 to 4 minutes until starting to soften.

Add the stock and let simmer for 5 to 10 minutes until the leeks and onion are tender. Add the cooked potatoes and nutmeg, and season to taste with salt and pepper.

Remove the pan from the heat and blend to a silky-smooth consistency using a hand-held stick blender, or blend in a food processor. Stir in the cream just before serving and heat through, if you like. If serving chilled, there is no need to warm the soup.

To serve, ladle the soup into bowls and scatter with the finely sliced leeks and crackers as a garnish.

Nutrition tip

Leeks are high in a fiber called inulin, which stimulates the growth of beneficial gut bacteria and helps keep your intestines healthy.

THIN THE SOUP with extra stock or water so it's easily sippable from a cup or glass, especially if serving chilled.

PLAIN YOGURT gives a lighter-tasting soup instead of the cream.

ADD a couple of chopped zucchini to boost the green vegetable content.

CARROT, ORANGE & CILANTRO SOUP

The flavors of orange, cilantro, and parsley have a natural affinity with carrot, and make this soup both comforting and fresh-tasting at the same time.

SERVES 4 TO 6

1 tablespoon olive oil or coconut oil

1 large onion, finely chopped ❄ 4 to 5 large carrots, grated

2½ cups hot Cooked Vegetable Stock (see page 15)

1 small bunch of parsley, leaves only

1 small bunch of cilantro, leaves only, plus extra to garnish

juice and finely grated zest of 1 large orange ❄ salt and pepper

Heat the oil in a large saucepan, add the onion, and sauté gently until lightly golden.

Add the carrots and stock and simmer for 10 to 15 minutes until softened.

Add the parsley leaves, cilantro leaves, and orange juice and zest. Blend to a smooth purée using a hand-held stick blender, or blend in a food processor. Add extra stock if you prefer a soup with a thinner consistency. Season to taste with salt and pepper.

To serve, ladle the soup into bowls and top with some extra chopped cilantro leaves.

Nutrition tip

You'll get all of your recommended daily allowance of vitamin A—important for the health of the immune system and skin—from this carroty soup.

FOR A SPICY SOUP, add ¼ teaspoon crushed coriander or cumin seeds to the onion before sautéing.

ADD a handful of grated carrot to give texture as well as extra nutrients and fiber.

IF YOU'RE USING organic carrots, chop a few of the fronds to scatter the top of the soup with.

ALKALIZING GREEN SOUP

This raw soup is wonderfully detoxifying and tastes delicious. I first saw a version of this soup in an amazing organic co-op in San Francisco called Rainbow Grocery and was compelled to make my own version when I got home.

SERVES 4 TO 6

1 large cucumber, coarsely chopped

2 to 3 zucchini, coarsely chopped

1 large ripe avocado, cut in half, seed removed, and flesh scooped out

5½ oz sugar snap peas, coarsely chopped

1 small bunch of kale, tough stalks removed

1 small bunch of parsley, leaves only

1 small bunch of cilantro, leaves only

Juice and finely grated zest of 1 lemon

1-inch piece fresh ginger root, peeled

1¼ cups filtered water ✳ salt and pepper

Place all the ingredients in a high-speed blender and blend until silky smooth. If the consistency is too thick, blend with a little more water. Chill for 2 to 3 hours, or until ready to eat, or blend with a handful of ice if you want to eat the soup immediately.

To serve, pour the soup into chilled glasses or bowls.

Nutrition tip

This raw soup is high in iron and vitamin C, and is totally alkaline—great as one of the dishes to eat following a juice cleanse.

✳

HEAT the soup gently to 113°F if you want to eat it warm but still keep it "raw."

TOP with a spoonful of Gazpacho Salsa (see page 135), or a dollop of raw almond cream.

CRAVE a bit of crunch? Serve with dehydrated vegetable chips or crackers.

GOLDEN BUTTERNUT SQUASH SOUP

This golden-hued soup is so thick and filling it makes a hearty main meal.
Sweet potatoes, pumpkin, or any other seasonal squash can be used instead
of the butternut squash.

SERVES 2 TO 3

3 large butternut squash, cut in half lengthwise and seeded ❊ 2 to 3 tablespoons olive oil

1 red bell pepper, seeded and cut into chunks ❊ 1 large onion, finely chopped

1 large carrot, thinly sliced ❊ 1 celery stalk, thinly sliced ❊ 3 garlic cloves, thinly sliced

¼ cup all-purpose flour ❊ 2½ cups hot Cooked Vegetable Stock (see page 15)

14 oz can diced tomatoes ❊ large pinch of dried chile flakes

1 teaspoon chopped thyme leaves ❊ salt and pepper

TO SERVE

Spiced Parsnip Chips (see page 134) ❊ Cajun spice mix

Sriracha Sauce (see page 135) ❊ Macadamia Cream Cheese (see page 137)

Preheat the oven to 325°F.

Place the squash on a roasting pan and drizzle with 1 tablespoon of the oil.
Season with salt and pepper and toss to coat. Roast the squash for 1 hour,
or until tender and slightly caramelized. Let cool slightly, then scoop the
squash out of the skins and purée it in a blender.

Heat the remaining oil in a saucepan, add the red bell pepper, onion, carrot, celery,
and garlic and fry gently until softened.

Remove the pan from the heat, add the flour, and stir well. Gradually add the stock, stirring
constantly, and then stir in the puréed squash, tomatoes, and chile flakes.

Return the pan to the heat and simmer for 20 minutes until warmed through and thickened,
adding extra stock to thin the soup if necessary. Add the thyme and check the seasoning.

To serve, ladle the soup into bowls and serve scattered with the parsnip chips and sprinkled
with Cajun spice mix. Finish with a drizzle of sriracha and macadamia cream cheese.

Nutrition tip

Red and orange vegetables provide a wealth of carotenoid and flavonoids, which have antioxidant and
anti-inflammatory effects. With a healthy dose or quercetin-rich garlic and onions, this soup
could help damp down minor allergies too.

SCATTER with crispy smoked pancetta and grated Parmesan cheese,
or try nutritional yeast flakes for a vegan alternative.

WATERMELON GAZPACHO

Serve this pretty, sweet, and spicy gazpacho as a summer appetizer. It also makes an extremely refreshing drink on its own, a little like watermelon limeade, or the base of a cocktail.

SERVES 4 TO 6

juice of 3 limes, skin removed, and fruit cut into chunks, seeds removed

1 large cucumber, chopped into large chunks

2 to 3 large red bell peppers, seeded and coarsely chopped

½ small red chile or jalapeño pepper, seeded and coarsely chopped

1 medium watermelon ❋ slices of lime and cucumber, to garnish

Run the lime, cucumber, red bell peppers, and chile through a juicer.

Cut the rind from the watermelon and cut the flesh into large chunks, removing the seeds. Place in a high-speed blender with the juiced fruit and vegetables and blend until smooth.

To serve, half-fill chilled glasses with ice, pour in the gazpacho, then garnish each serving with a twist of cucumber and a slice of lime.

Nutrition tip

This slimline soup will hydrate you and is a good source of the antioxidant lycopene, which has been linked with good cardiovascular health.

FREEZE in ice-cube trays and use as flavored ice in drinks or chilled soups or freeze into ice pops, sorbet, or granita.

A SHOT of vodka turns the soup into a vibrant summer cocktail.

TOMATO CAULI RICE SOUP

This is a simple raw soup made from a savory juice that can be warmed gently if you don't like the thought of eating it cold. The "riced" zucchini and cauliflower add some texture—a welcome addition if you're in the middle of a juice cleanse.

SERVES 3 TO 4

½ head of cauliflower, outer leaves removed, broken into florets

1 large zucchini, coarsely chopped

6 to 8 large ripe tomatoes, coarsely chopped

2 large red bell peppers, seeded and finely chopped

2 large carrots, coarsely chopped ✳ 2 celery stalks, coarsely chopped

½ red onion, coarsely chopped ✳ ½ garlic clove, peeled

salt and pepper

Place the cauliflower and zucchini in the bowl of a food processor and blitz into ricelike grains. Spread the mixture out onto paper towels to absorb any excess moisture.

Run the rest of the ingredients through a juicer and season to taste with salt and pepper.

To serve, place a couple of spoons of the vegetable rice into bowls and ladle in some savory juice.

Nutrition tip

Cauliflower is part of the cruciferous family of vegetables, and consuming it has been linked with lower risk of some cancers.

❋

HEAT the soup gently to 113°F if you want to eat it warm but still keep it "raw."

STIR-FRY the cauliflower and zucchini "rice," then drizzle it with a little of the warmed juice to make an interesting side dish.

STIR IN shredded carrot or finely diced red bell pepper for extra texture.

ASPARAGUS & FENNEL SOUP

This light, delicate soup is good served warm or chilled and is at its best when asparagus is in season and plentiful.

SERVES 3 TO 4

10 to 12 asparagus spears, woody ends broken off

1 large fennel bulb, coarsely chopped, fronds reserved

3 to 4 scallions, coarsely chopped

1¾ cups hot Cooked Vegetable Stock (see page 15)

juice and finely grated zest of 1 lemon ❋ salt and pepper

1 small rosemary sprig, needles very finely chopped, to garnish

Set aside 2 asparagus spears and coarsely chop the remainder. Place the chopped asparagus, fennel, scallions, and stock in a large saucepan and simmer for 20 to 25 minutes until the vegetables are tender. You can also sauté the vegetables briefly in a little oil before adding the stock, but this will result in a slightly darker soup.

Remove the pan from the heat and purée the soup until smooth using a hand-held stick blender, or blend in a high-speed blender, adding more stock if necessary. Add the lemon juice and zest and season to taste with salt and pepper.

Cut the reserved asparagus spears into fine disks or shave into long ribbons with a vegetable peeler.

To serve, ladle the soup into bowls and serve scattered with the reserved fennel fronds, rosemary, and disks or ribbons of raw asparagus.

Nutrition tip

There's no vegetable richer in folic acid—needed for manufacturing red blood cells—than fresh asparagus. This soup is also good for your digestive system, with soothing fennel and prebiotic fiber.

SERVE chilled on a hot day, topped with a swirl of sour cream and a few ice cubes.

FRESH MINT, tarragon, or dill would all be good substitutes for the rosemary.

COOK slices of Parma ham or prosciutto in a dry skillet until crisp then crumble it on top of the soup for a savory meaty garnish.

CARROT, COUSCOUS & CHARD SOUP

I've used giant couscous because the larger grains are more robust in this rustic soup-cum-stew. The standard couscous works, too, but just be careful not to overcook it. I sauté the carrot ribbons briefly to keep an element of crunch, but you could cook them for longer and then blend all the cooked vegetables together and serve the couscous stirred in at the end.

SERVES 3 TO 4

7oz giant Israeli couscous ❋ 2²⁄₃ cups hot Cooked Vegetable Stock (see page 15)

2 tablespoons olive oil or coconut oil ❋ 2 teaspoons Dukkah (see page 128), plus extra for sprinkling

1 large onion, coarsely chopped ❋ 2 celery stalks, coarsely chopped

2 garlic cloves, finely chopped

1 large bunch of rainbow chard, stems and leaves separated, and coarsely chopped

2 to 3 large carrots, preferably purple, sliced with a vegetable peeler into thin ribbons

Pour the couscous into a large saucepan and lightly toast the grains over medium-high heat, stirring often. Pour in the stock, stir, and simmer for 10 to 15 minutes until the couscous is cooked through. Take the pan off the heat and set aside.

While the couscous is cooking, heat the oil in a large sauté pan, add the dukkah, onion, celery, garlic, and chard stems, and sauté gently until softened.

Add the chard leaves and carrots and cook gently until softened slightly and the chard leaves have wilted. Add them to the pan with the couscous and stock and simmer briefly until heated through.

To serve, ladle the soup into bowls and serve sprinkled with a little extra dukkah.

Nutrition tip

This soup provides a healthy balance of vegetables and carbohydrates—serve with cheese or spicy sausage as suggested to turn it into a completely balanced meal.

❋

SERVE with thick slices of toasted country-style bread.
CRUMBLE a little goat cheese or feta on the top just before serving.
FOR NONVEGETARIANS, add cooked, sliced spicy rustic sausage.

BEET & BARBERRY SOUP

The sweetness of the beets in this soup is tempered by the sour flavor of the dried barberries and the spiciness of the horseradish cream. Barberries are small red berries that are often used in Iranian cooking, and add a slight sharpness to the flavor. Dried unsweetened cranberries make a good substitute. Serve warm or chilled.

SERVES 3 TO 4

4 to 5 large raw beets with leaves, stalks and leaves removed and reserved, to garnish

1¾ cups hot Cooked Vegetable Stock (see page 15) ❋ 2 tablespoons dried barberries

squeeze of lemon juice (optional) ❋ salt and pepper

TO SERVE

½ teaspoon grated fresh horseradish

3 tablespoons Raw Almond Yogurt (see page 137) or Raw Cashew Cream (see page 138)

2 tablespoons flaked almonds

wheat crackers or lightly toasted rye bread

Place the beets in a large saucepan of boiling salted water and cook, uncovered, for about 30 to 40 minutes until tender. Remove the beets and set aside until cool enough to handle. When cool, peel off the skins (wearing rubber gloves is advisable) and chop the flesh into large chunks.

Using a hand-held stick blender or high-speed blender, purée the cooked beets with the stock and half the barberries until a thick, smooth consistency. Season to taste with salt and pepper, and add a squeeze of lemon juice if the soup is too sweet.

Before serving, mix the horseradish with the yogurt or cream. Toast the flaked almonds in a dry skillet for 3 to 4 minutes until lightly golden. Finely chop the reserved beet leaves.

To serve, ladle the soup into bowls and top with a spoonful of the horseradish cream, beet leaves, flaked almonds, and the remaining barberries. Serve with a few wheat crackers or lightly toasted rye bread, if you like.

Nutrition tip

Beets are naturally rich in nitrates, which the body uses to make the nitric oxide, which can lower blood pressure and optimize physical performance.

FLAKED cooked salmon, smoked trout or mackerel, or slices of gravadlax make a delicious fishy topping.

DICED hard-boiled eggs or some salty feta or goat cheese all team well with cooked beets.

INSTEAD OF the beet leaves, use chopped chives or watercress as a green garnish.

USE any leftover beet stems and leaves in a salad, or sauté the leaves like spinach, or juice them. Just don't throw them away because they're full of goodness.

SPIRALIZED ZUCCHINI & KALE SOUP

The spiralized zucchini adds a great textural element to this soup. I only partially cooked it so it's still al dente (cooking spiralized zucchini for too long makes it limp and watery), but you could blitz the whole thing together to make a smooth blended soup. The sautéed cavolo nero gives a savory "meaty" flavor to the dish and the toasted pine nuts add crunch.

SERVES 3 TO 4

2 to 3 zucchini, spiralized or cut into julienne strips ✳ 1 tablespoon olive oil or coconut oil

4 to 5 cavolo nero leaves, or the equivalent amount of kale, stalks discarded
and leaves torn into large pieces

2½ cups Passata (see page 138) or Three Tomato Soup (see page 86)

pinch of sumac ✳ salt and pepper

¼ cup toasted pine nuts, to serve

Blanch the spiralized zucchini briefly in boiling water until just softened, then drain
and place on paper towels until required.

Heat the oil in a large sauté pan, add the cavolo nero, and sauté until wilted and softened.

Pour the passata into a saucepan and heat gently. Add the spiralized zucchini and cavolo
nero and heat until warmed through. Season to taste with salt and pepper.

To serve, ladle the soup into bowls, add a pinch of sumac to each one,
and scatter with the pine nuts.

Nutrition tip

Kale is super-rich in vitamin C and lutein (good for eyes),
while zucchini provides potassium, folic acid, and vitamin A.

SCATTER with a handful of grated Parmesan cheese just before serving.
CHOPPED sun-dried tomatoes add an extra-rich tomato flavor.
SAUTÉED cubes of pancetta or chorizo work well with the tomato-based soup.
STIR IN barbecued shrimp or chicken.

RAW AVOCADO & CUCUMBER SOUP

This raw soup is really refreshing on a hot day, and the chives give a gentle onion flavor without being too overpowering. The chilled cucumber pearls make an attractive garnish. However, if you don't have a mini melon baller, or the time or patience to make them, dice the cucumber instead. It'll taste just the same!

SERVES 3 TO 4

2 large ripe avocados, cut in half, stones removed, and flesh scooped out

2 large cucumbers, peeled if not organic, and coarsely chopped

juice of 1 lemon ❋ ½ cup cold water

1 small bunch of chives, snipped ❋ salt and pepper

TO SERVE

1 cucumber, cut in half lengthwise

½ avocado, seed removed, peeled and diced

Place all the ingredients, except the garnish (and reserving a few chives to garnish), in a high-speed blender and blitz until silky smooth. You may need to add a little extra water, depending on how juicy your cucumbers are. Season to taste with salt and pepper.

Before serving, make the cucumber pearls. Using a mini melon baller, scoop out small balls of cucumber, avoiding the seedy part running down the center. (Save any leftover cucumber to use in a juice or chop into a salad.)

To serve, ladle the soup into chilled bowls or glasses and top with the diced avocado, cucumber pearls, and the reserved snipped chives.

Nutrition tip

Avocados provide good monunsaturated fats, which are the type that reduce cholesterol. They're also a really good source of vitamin E and some B vitamins.

A HANDFUL of chopped tomatoes gives an additional savory flavor.

BLEND in a few sprigs of fresh cilantro for an herbal boost.

FREEZE the blended soup to make a savory ice cream, and serve in scoops in chilled bowls or glasses.

GAZPACHO

This chilled soup is really easy to make and is best enjoyed in summer when tomatoes are at their best and most flavorsome. Some gazpacho recipes call for the addition of stale bread, but I prefer to keep my version simply fresh fruit and vegetables. Serve it with a crunchy salsa topping—made out of the same ingredients as the soup—to add texture to this otherwise smooth soup.

SERVES 3 TO 4

1 cucumber, coarsely chopped

2¾ cups coarsely chopped ripe tomatoes

1 red bell pepper, seeded and coarsely chopped

3 celery stalks, coarsely chopped ❋ 3 to 4 scallions, coarsely chopped

2 small garlic cloves, coarsely chopped

1 small handful of parsley or basil leaves

1 tablespoon olive oil, plus extra for drizzling ❋ ½ cup water

salt and pepper ❋ Gazpacho Salsa, to serve (see page 135)

Place all the ingredients in a high-speed blender, then blend until smooth, adding a little extra water if needed. Season to taste with salt and pepper.

Cover the soup and let chill in the fridge for 2 to 3 hours, or until ready to serve.

To serve, ladle the soup into bowls, top with the gazpacho salsa, and drizzle with some extra olive oil.

Nutrition tip

The tomatoes in gazpacho give you a great boost of the antioxidant lycopene. As well as being cardio-protective, lycopene may offer some protection for skin against UV damage.

❋

IF PREFERRED, serve the soup warm. Heat it gently, but don't overheat it or the soup will turn watery and lose its fresh flavor.

FOR a Bloody Mary-type twist, add a couple of shots of good vodka.

A PINCH of hot paprika or a few drops of Worcestershire sauce or Tabasco would give a spicy hit.

BUTTERNUT NOODLE SOUP

I like this vegetable-dense soup served chunky so it's more like a stew, but you can also blend the green vegetables into a sauce to serve over the butternut squash noodles. I've caramelized the onions to give a crispy, sweet finish and have added a pinch of panch phoran (an Indian whole spice mix) for a hint of curry flavor.

SERVES 3 TO 4

2 tablespoons olive oil or coconut oil ✳ 2 red onions, very finely sliced

1 teaspoon sugar or maple syrup, or sweetener of choice

pinch of Panch Phoran (see page 128) ✳ 2 garlic cloves, finely chopped

1 leek, finely chopped ✳ 2 large zucchini, diced into small cubes

4 to 5 cavolo nero leaves or the equivalent of kale, stalks removed
and leaves torn into large pieces

3 to 4 scallions, finely chopped ✳ 2½ cups hot Cooked Vegetable Stock (see page 15)

1 large butternut squash, peeled and spiralized, or cut into julienne strips

1 small handful of parsley leaves, coarsely chopped ✳ salt and pepper

First caramelize the red onions. Heat 1 tablespoon of the oil in a large sauté pan, add the onions, sugar, and a pinch of salt and cook, stirring frequently, over medium-high heat for 10 minutes, or until the onions are cooked, crisp, and golden. Transfer from the pan onto a plate lined with paper towels and set aside.

Heat the remaining oil in the sauté pan or a saucepan, add the panch phoran, and cook briefly until the spices release their fragrance and start to pop.

Stir in the garlic, leek, and zucchini and sauté gently until the vegetables soften. Add the cavolo nero and scallions and cook for a further 5 minutes until wilted and softened.

Pour in the stock and add the butternut squash, cover, and simmer for 5 to 10 minutes until the "noodles" are tender. Stir in the parsley and season to taste with salt and pepper.

To serve, ladle the soup into bowls and scatter with the caramelized onions.

Nutrition tip

Orange-hued butternut squash provides lots of carotenoid antioxidants. If you're keeping an eye on your weight, it's more waistline-friendly than sweet potato.

A COUPLE of softly poached or fried eggs on top make a more substantial meal.
ADD cooked flaked white fish or salmon for extra protein, or scatter with toasted nuts and seeds.
TURN the "noodles" into a type of rösti instead of a soup, and serve with the greens on top.

HIDDEN VEGETABLE SOUP

Adding raw grated vegetables is an easy way to bulk up a cooked meal, as well as give it texture. It's also a good option if you want to disguise vegetables from vegetable-haters, young or old! I've used little star-shaped pasta, stelline, as it cooks really quickly, while ready-made passata (see page 138) makes a convenient base and speeds up the preparation time, too. I often add lemon juice or zest to tomato-based sauces and soups to give a brightness and freshness of flavor. Adding a pinch of sumac has a similar effect.

SERVES 3 TO 4

3½ to 4½oz dried pasta, such as stelline, orzo, trofie, or short-cut macaroni

2 cups passata ✳ 1 large zucchini, coarsely grated

1 large carrot, coarsely grated

1 small handful of mixed herbs, such as basil, parsley, thyme,
oregano, and marjoram, finely chopped

few pinches of sumac ✳ salt and pepper

Cook the dried pasta following the package directions, then drain and set aside.

While the pasta is cooking, pour the passata into a large saucepan and add the grated zucchini and carrot, then simmer for 5 to 10 minutes until the vegetables have softened but are still al dente.

Stir in the herbs and cooked pasta. Season to taste with salt and pepper, then simmer for a few more minutes until heated through.

To serve, ladle the soup into bowls and sprinkle with a pinch of sumac.

Nutrition tip

Fresh herbs bump up the health value of any dish, adding antioxidants, vitamin K, and vitamin C.

BEETS, sweet potatoes, parsnips, or red bell peppers also work well in this soup.

INCLUDE cubes of cooked ham or marinated tofu for added protein.

A HANDFUL of grated Parmesan cheese and/or a dollop of pesto make great toppings.

STIR IN a spoonful of Raw Cashew Cream (see page 138), cream, or crème fraîche for a rich, soup with a creamy texture.

MIXED MUSHROOM SOUP

I've used a combination of different mushrooms, including cremino mushrooms and fresh wild morels (though you could also use cultivated ones). They have a rich, earthy taste and a few wild mushrooms always go a long way flavorwise.

SERVES 3 TO 4

2 tablespoons olive oil ❋ 1 onion, finely chopped

1 leek, finely chopped ❋ 2 garlic cloves, finely chopped

1lb 2oz mixed mushrooms, cleaned and coarsely chopped, plus extra to serve

2½ cups hot Cooked Vegetable Stock (see page 15)

2 to 3 thyme sprigs, leaves stripped ❋ 1 bay leaf

3 tablespoons Raw Cashew Cream (see page 138) or crème fraîche

salt and pepper

Heat the oil in a large saucepan, add the onion, leek, and garlic and sauté gently until softened.

Add the mushrooms and some salt and pepper and cook for 5 to 10 minutes until tender. Add the stock, thyme, and bay leaf and let simmer for 30 minutes.

Remove the pan from the heat, remove the bay leaf, and stir in the cashew cream. Blend the soup until smooth and creamy using a hand-held stick blender, then check the seasoning and add more salt or pepper, if needed.

To serve, ladle the soup into bowls and scatter with a few finely sliced fresh mushrooms.

Nutrition tip

Mushrooms are a good source of B vitamins, which help our cells release energy from food. Set them gill-side up on a sunny windowsill before using and they'll be a good source vitamin D, too.

❋

TRY ADDING a small handful of soaked dried mushrooms, such as porcini, for an extra mushroomy flavor boost.

ADD A handful of cooked barley, brown rice, or lentils for a hearty rustic meal.

A GLUG of Marsala wine adds a rich, luxuriant touch to this soup.

SPRING VEGETABLE SOUP

This soup can be made with any new-season spring vegetables. I've used ramsons becaus they grow in profusion where I live, as well as monk's beard (also known as agretti). I love its fresh minerally taste and crisp succulent texture. Monk's beard looks similar to chives, but its overriding flavor is similar to a combination of samphire, asparagus, and spinach, all of which can be used as substitutions.

To reduce dishwashing, this soup can be made in a multi-tier steamer. Cook the potatoes in the stock at the bottom, and let the green vegetables steam above.

SERVES 2 TO 3

½ lb baby new potatoes, halved

4 to 5 ramson leaves, plus flowers to garnish, or 2 garlic cloves, peeled and left whole

2½ cups hot Cooked Vegetable Stock (see page 15)

½ large head of broccoli, broken into small florets

2 large handfuls of monk's beard, samphire, baby spinach, or
asparagus spears, woody ends broken off

salt and pepper ✳ Fresh Herb Pesto (see page 135), to serve

Place the new potatoes and garlic cloves, if using instead of ramsons, in a saucepan or in the bottom of a multi-tier steamer and add the stock. Bring to a simmer, then place the broccoli and monk's beard in the steamer containers above; the monk's beard will take the least time to cook so put this at the very top. Steam the green vegetables until they're just cooked and simmer the potatoes until they're tender.

(If you don't have a steamer, boil the potatoes and garlic, cook the broccoli in a separate pan for 4 to 5 minutes, and the monk's beard in a third pan for 2 to 3 minutes.)

Remove half of the potatoes from the stock and set aside. Tip the broccoli into the pan with the remaining potatoes and the ramsons, if using instead of the whole cloves, and blitz with a hand-held stick blender to make a finely textured soup. (Alternatively, blend the mixture in a food processor).

To serve, ladle the soup into bowls, add the reserved potatoes and monk's beard, and a dollop of fresh herb pesto. Finally, scatter with a few ramson flowers, if you have them.

Nutrition tip

This soup has lots of heart-healthy ingredients, including potassium, folic acid, and sulfur compounds provided by the garlic.

TRY WITH baby zucchini, leeks, and peas instead.
ADD a handful of cooked beans or pasta for a minestrone-style soup.
SHREDDED cooked chicken or lamb would make a more substantial soup.

BLACK BEAN SOUP

I love the sinister jet-black color of this soup, and it makes such a great foil to any brightly colored toppings. I've used avocado, hemp seeds, and candy cane beet, but a dollop of sour cream, the sliced green part of a scallion, diced orange bell pepper, or kernel corn would all stand out brilliantly against this very dark soup.

SERVES 3 TO 4

1 cup dried black beans ❄ 1 bay leaf

1 small onion, cut in half ❄ 2 garlic cloves, peeled and left whole

1 small dried red chile

2½ cups hot Cooked Vegetable Stock (see page 15)

salt and pepper

Put the beans in a bowl and cover with plenty of cold water. Let soak overnight, then drain.

Place the beans in a large saucepan with the bay leaf, onion, garlic, and chile and cover with fresh cold water. Bring to a boil, then turn the heat down and let simmer, partly covered, for about 1 hour, or until tender. When cooked, drain the beans, discard the bay leaf, onion, garlic, and chile and set aside.

To make the soup, return the beans to the pan, pour in the stock, and part-blend the beans using a hand-held stick blender. (Keep some of them whole for a chunky texture.) Season to taste with salt and pepper.

To serve, ladle the soup into bowls and add the fixin's of your choice.

Nutrition tip

Black beans are super beans, packed with protein and cell-protective antioxidants (it's the antioxidant components that make them so dark in color).

SPEED UP the preparation time by using canned black beans.

ADD some crumbled crispy bacon or barbecued pulled pork for a more substantial meal.

A SPRINKLING of grated Cheddar cheese increases the protein content.

PURPLE POTATO SOUP

I love colorful vegetables and when I find purple potatoes I can't resist buying them. This soup is made using a French variety called Vitelotte, which have an almost black skin, a violet-blue flesh, and a nutty flavor like chestnuts. You can, of course, use any type of potato, but those with a dense texture work best in this soup.

SERVES 3 TO 4

2 tablespoons vegan butter

1 large onion, finely chopped ✳ 1 celery stalk, finely chopped

2 to 3 garlic cloves, finely chopped, or 4 to 5 ramson leaves,
plus extra to garnish

1lb 2oz purple potatoes, cut into large chunks

2¾ cups hot Cooked Vegetable Stock (see page 15) ✳ salt and pepper

purple Oven-baked Potato Chips (see page 132), to serve

Melt the butter in a large saucepan, add the onion, celery, and garlic cloves, if using instead of the ramsons, and sauté gently until softened.

Add the potatoes and stock and simmer for 15 to 20 minutes until the potatoes are tender and start to break apart. Add the ramsons, if using instead of the cloves.

Remove the pan from the heat and blend until smooth using a hand-held stick blender, adding more stock, if necessary. Season to taste with salt and pepper.

To serve, ladle the soup into bowls and garnish with a few shredded ramson leaves and flowers, if you have them. Serve with purple potato chips on the side.

Nutrition tip

Purple potatoes have the benefit of being a good source of anthoycanins, which research suggests may be important for cardiovascular health and good cognitive function.

✳

INSTEAD of the ramsons, serve the soup with a dollop of sour cream and a few chopped scallions on top.

FOR A DOUBLE DOSE of purple, add some chopped purple heritage carrots at the same time as the potatoes—you may need to add extra stock.

ROAST the vegetables, rather than simmer them, for a more intensely flavored, sweeter soup.

ADD 1 cup nut milk or Raw Cashew Cream (see page 138) for a luxurious soup with a rich taste.

CELERY SOUP

Even those who dislike celery usually love this soup! The flavor of the celery mellows with cooking and is softened by the addition of sour cream and spiked with a hit of spice from the pink peppercorns. Celery is naturally salty, so you won't need much seasoning.

SERVES 2 TO 3

1 tablespoon olive oil ❋ 1 large onion, finely chopped

2 to 3 garlic cloves, finely chopped

1 bunch of celery, stalks separated and thinly sliced, leaves reserved

2½ cups hot Cooked Vegetable Stock (see page 15)

1 to 2 teaspoons pink peppercorns, crushed

½ cup Raw Sour Cashew Cream (see page 138) or crème fraîche, plus extra to serve

salt and pepper

Heat the oil in a large saucepan, add the onion and garlic, and fry gently for a few minutes until softened but not colored.

Add the celery and stock and simmer for 15 to 20 minutes, or until the celery is soft and cooked through.

Add the soup to a food processor and blitz to a blended but still slightly chunky texture, or use a hand-held stick blender to purée to a smooth consistency.

Stir the pink peppercorns into the soup with the sour cream.
Season to taste with salt and pepper.

To serve, ladle the soup into bowls before scattering with the reserved celery leaves and drizzling with sour cream.

Nutrition tip

This potassium-rich soup is also a good source of iron if you top it with the cashew cream.

A BLUE-VEINED CHEESE, such as Stilton or Roquefort, tastes great crumbled into this soup.
STIR shredded cooked chicken or fresh crabmeat into the soup.
GRATED apple adds a slight sweetness and marries well with the flavor of the celery.

FARRO & PINK RADICCHIO SOUP

Pink radicchio, typically grown in Verona, in Italy, is sweeter and less bitter than traditional radicchio, and is great to serve raw in a salad or soup. I've teamed it with farro, a chewy, nutty-tasting grain that works well with the slightly bitter radicchio. Just add extra stock if you prefer a consistency more like broth.

SERVES 3 TO 4

2 tablespoons olive oil ❋ 1 small carrot, finely chopped

1 onion, finely chopped ❋ 1 cup farro

2 cups hot Cooked Vegetable Stock (see page 15)

2 pink radicchio, tough stems removed, leaves separated, large ones cut in half

juice and finely grated zest of 1 orange ❋ salt and pepper

Heat the oil in a large saucepan, add the carrot and onion, and cook gently for a few minutes until softened but not colored.

Stir in the farro then cook briefly for 2 to 3 minutes before adding the stock. Bring to a boil, then turn the heat down and simmer for 15 minutes. Add the radicchio and cook for a further 5 to 10 minutes until it has wilted and the farro is tender

Stir in the orange juice and most of the zest, reserving a little to garnish, and season to taste with salt and pepper.

To serve, ladle the soup into bowls and sprinkle with the reserved orange zest.

Nutrition tip

Farro is slightly lower in gluten than many grains and people with mild gluten intolerances can often find it easier to digest.

BROWN OR WILD RICE OR PEARL BARLEY would be good substitutes, if you can't get hold of farro.

TURN the soup into a pink radicchio salad instead. Simply mix the radicchio leaves with the cooked farro, onion, and carrot and serve it with an orange juice and sumac dressing.

SUNSHINE SOUP

The cheery sunshine yellow color of this soup comes from the yellow bell peppers and zucchini. I've blended it in a food processor to keep it slightly chunky. This is a great soup to make in the summer when zucchini and bell peppers are plentiful.

SERVES 3 TO 4

1 tablespoon olive oil or coconut oil ✳ 1 onion, finely chopped

1 small carrot, finely chopped ✳ 2 celery stalks, finely chopped

4 to 5 yellow zucchini, cut into large chunks

2 yellow bell peppers, seeded and finely chopped

3¼ cups hot Cooked Vegetable Stock (see page 15)

1 small handful of parsley leaves, coarsely chopped

salt and pepper

TO SERVE

1 green zucchini ✳ 1 yellow zucchini

Heat the oil in a large saucepan and add the onion, carrot, and celery. Fry gently for a few minutes until softened but not colored.

Stir in the zucchini, bell peppers, and stock, season with salt and pepper, and let simmer gently for 10 to 15 minutes, or until the zucchini are tender.

Add the soup to a food processor and blend briefly, keeping it slightly chunky.

Before serving, prepare the zucchini garnish by scoring the skin of the green and yellow zucchini lengthwise to make shallow, v-shaped grooves. Then slice very thinly crosswise.

To serve, ladle the soup into bowls and scatter with the parsley and zucchini "flowers."

Nutrition tip

Yellow bell peppers contain good amounts of lutein and zeaxanthin, which are antioxidants that can help protect the back of the eye from UV damage.

✳

FOR EXTRA SUBSTANCE, add a few handfuls of cooked grains, such as brown rice, farro, or bulgur wheat, or add some cooked pasta.

A DOLLOP of red or green pesto boosts the Mediterranean flavor of the soup.

COCONUT CAULIFLOWER SOUP

This is a great recipe for cauliflower lovers because it gives a double hit of the vegetable. I think it could win over any cauliflower haters as well, as the smooth and creamy soup is enhanced with coconut milk and fragrant lime leaves. What's more, the crispy pan-fried cauliflower steaks are nothing like cauliflower as we know it!

SERVES 3 TO 4

1 large cauliflower, outer leaves and tough core removed and cut into large chunks

1 to 2 tablespoons coconut oil ❋ 1 garlic clove, finely chopped

3 to 4 kaffir lime leaves, finely chopped ❋ 1½ to 1¾ cups coconut milk

1¼ cups hot Quick "No-Recipe" Light Vegetable Stock (see page 16)

juice and finely grated zest of 1 lime

salt and pepper ❋ Cauliflower Steaks, to serve (see page 134)

Place the cauliflower in a food processor and blitz to very small grains without letting it turn to mush.

Heat the coconut oil in a large saucepan, add the cauliflower, and stir-fry for 1 to 2 minutes over high heat without coloring.

Reduce the heat, add the garlic and lime leaves, then pour in the coconut milk and stock. Let simmer gently until the cauliflower is cooked through and forms a soft, pulpy soup. If you prefer a thinner consistency, add a little extra coconut milk, water, or stock.

Stir in the lime juice and zest and season to taste with salt and pepper.

To serve, ladle the soup into bowls and top each serving with a cauliflower steak.

Nutrition tip

Cruciferous vegetables like cauliflower are on a list of "foods that fight cancer" produced by the American Institute for Cancer Research. Cauliflower is also a good source of pantothenic acid, a B vitamin that helps release energy from the food we eat.

A HANDFUL of chopped cilantro adds an herbal freshness.
BLEND the cauliflower steaks into the soup to give a subtle smoky taste.
USE LESS stock and serve as a side dish to a main meal, such as roast chicken.

WHITE BEAN & RADICCHIO SOUP

Even though this soup is more of a plant-based stew, it becomes a beautiful creamy, pale-pink color when blended. The creaminess and mild flavor of the beans complement and temper the slight bitterness of the radicchio.

SERVES 4 TO 5

2 cup dried navy beans, rinsed and drained

1 small onion, cut in half ✳ 2 thyme sprigs

2 garlic cloves, peeled ✳ 1 tablespoon olive oil

2 radicchio, tough stems removed, leaves separated, larger ones cut in half

3½ cups hot Quick "No-Recipe" Light Vegetable Stock (see page 16)

salt and pepper

TO SERVE

1 small handful of chopped herbs or micro herbs ✳ sprouted seeds or pea shoots

Put the beans in a bowl and cover with plenty of cold water. Let soak overnight, then drain.

Place the beans in a large saucepan with the onion, thyme, and garlic and cover with fresh cold water. Bring to a boil, then turn the heat down and simmer for about 1 hour, or until tender. Drain, discarding the thyme, garlic, and onion, and keep the beans warm until ready to use.

Heat the oil in a large sauté pan and add the radicchio. Stir and cook briefly over medium-high heat until the leaves have wilted. Pour in ½ cup of the stock, cover with the lid, and simmer gently for 10 minutes, or until the radicchio is cooked through. Add the cooked beans to the pan with the remaining stock.

Remove the pan from the heat and blend until smooth and creamy using a hand-held stick blender. Season to taste with salt and pepper.

To serve, ladle the soup into bowls and scatter each serving with the herbs and sprouted seeds or pea shoots.

Nutrition tip

Radicchio contains good levels of lutein and vitamin E, while you'll get a good level of magnesium—important for energy production and a healthy nervous system—from the navy beans.

SHORT OF TIME? Try using canned navy beans instead.

SERVE sprinkled with grated Parmesan or cheese-flavored nutritional yeast flakes.

STIR IN some finely shredded raw radicchio just before serving, and add a dollop of pesto for extra color, texture, and flavor.

NONVEGETARIANS may like to add cooked diced chorizo.

THREE TOMATO SOUP

This simple soup uses three different types of tomatoes as well as garlic and fresh herbs. You could also add some tomato paste to give it another layer of tomato flavor.

SERVES 3 TO 4

1 small handful of sun-dried tomatoes, coarsely chopped

2 tablespoons olive oil ✳ 2 onions, finely chopped

3 to 4 garlic cloves, finely chopped ✳ 10½oz ripe tomatoes

1⅔ cups canned diced tomatoes ✳ pinch of sugar

1 large handful of mixed herbs, such as thyme, oregano, marjoram, sage, and basil, plus extra to garnish

salt and pepper

Place the sun-dried tomatoes in a bowl and add boiling water to cover. Add a pinch of salt and let stand for 20 to 30 minutes until softened, then drain.

Heat the oil in a large saucepan, add the onions and garlic, and sauté gently until softened.

Add the drained sun-dried and fresh tomatoes and simmer for 10 to 15 minutes until the fresh tomatoes have softened and released their juices. Stir in the canned tomatoes, sugar, and herbs. Season to taste with salt and pepper, and simmer for a further 10 minutes.

Remove the pan from the heat. Blend the mixture until smooth using a hand-held stick blender, or blend in a food processor. Or, leave it slightly chunky for a more rustic texture.

To serve, ladle the soup into bowls and serve scattered with a few extra fresh herbs.

Nutrition tip

You'll get a big boost of tomato lycopene from this soup. Studies suggest this could help reduce your risk of heart disease and potentially protect your skin against UV damage, too.

SPOON the soup over grilled country bread rubbed with garlic or just serve with toasted crusty bread.

SERVE as a pasta sauce, or as the base for a Bolognese or ragù sauce.

FOR EXTRA SUBSTANCE, stir in a handful of long-grain rice, add about 1 cup water, and let simmer until the rice is cooked.

KERNEL CORN SOUP

This golden-yellow soup is very creamy, even without the addition of any dairy products. The acidity of the balsamic vinegar cuts through the natural sweetness of the corn helping to balance out the flavors. Serve warm or chilled.

SERVES 2 TO 3

4 cobs of corn, husks stripped off ❋ 1 tablespoon olive oil

1 onion, finely chopped ❋ 2 garlic cloves, finely chopped

2 celery stalks, finely chopped ❋ 1 white potato, peeled and finely chopped

1 teaspoon thyme leaves ❋ 2 cups hot Cooked Vegetable Stock (see page 15)

1 tablespoon balsamic vinegar ❋ salt and pepper

Stand a cob of corn upright on a cutting board and slice off the kernels in a downward motion. Repeat with the remaining corn cobs.

Toast one-quarter of the kernels in a large, dry, nonstick skillet for 4 to 5 minutes until golden and crisp. Set aside until ready to serve the soup.

Heat the oil in a large saucepan or sauté pan, add the onion, garlic, and celery and fry gently until softened.

Add the potato, remaining raw corn kernels, thyme, and stock. Bring to a boil, cover, and then let it bubble away gently for 20 to 30 minutes or until the potato is cooked through.

Remove the pan from the heat and blend the soup until smooth and creamy using a hand-held stick blender, or add it to a food processor and blend lightly for a slightly chunkier texture. Season to taste with salt and pepper.

To serve, ladle the soup into bowls, scatter with the toasted corn, and drizzle with the balsamic vinegar.

Nutrition tip

Yellow corn is a good source of lutein and zeaxanthin, antioxidants that are associated, in particular, with good eye health.

ADD cooked seafood, such as shrimp, crab, squid, clams, or smoked haddock, to create the flavors of a traditional chowder.

FROZEN OR CANNED kernel corn can be used instead of fresh.

SWEET POTATO SOUP

This makes a beautiful deep-golden soup; I like to set its color off with a contrasting purple topping. I've used finely shredded radicchio and purple-tinged mint leaves in the photograph, but purple basil or chopped red chard stems, purple shiso leaves, or sprouting beet seeds all look beautiful, too.

I've also added a topping of grated raw sweet potato because it's surprisingly good eaten raw and gives a contrast in texture to the velvety smooth soup. The spiced crispy chickpeas are a great alternative to crunchy bread croutons.

SERVES 4

2 tablespoons olive oil or coconut oil ❋ 1 large white or red onion, finely chopped

2 to 3 garlic cloves, finely chopped ❋ 1 teaspoon ras-el-hanout spice mix, plus extra for sprinkling

3 large sweet potatoes, peeled and coarsely grated

1 quart hot Cooked Vegetable Stock (see page 15) ❋ 2 tablespoons tahini

salt and pepper

TO SERVE

Spiced Roasted Chickpeas (see page 134)

1 handful of purple mint leaves ❋ few radicchio leaves, shredded

Heat the oil in a large saucepan, add the onion and garlic, and fry gently until softened. Then add the ras-el-hanout and cook, stirring, for a further few minutes, or until the spices release their fragrance.

Add the sweet potatoes, reserving a little to garnish, and stock. Bring to a boil, then turn the heat down and simmer for 10 to 15 minutes, or until the sweet potatoes are tender and cooked through. Stir in the tahini.

Remove the pan from the heat and blend until silky smooth using a hand-held stick blender, or blend in a food processor.

Ladle the soup into bowls and top with the roasted chickpeas, the reserved grated sweet potato, and an extra sprinkling of ras-el-hanout. Scatter with herbs and radicchio to serve.

Nutrition tip

Full of slow-release energy, sweet potatoes are higher in vitamins C and E than normal potatoes. In addition, the yellow color denotes beta-carotene, which the body can use to make vitamin A.

STIR IN some cooked shredded chicken or pulled pork to turn this into a more substantial meal.
ADD cooked mini lamb and mint meatballs and a handful of cooked couscous for a Moroccan-type stew.

RED LENTIL SOUP

This is a simple, comforting soup that you can cook quickly because the lentils don't need presoaking. If you don't like it too spicy, reduce the amount of dried and fresh chile, or omit them. I've served the soup with roasted caramelized carrots and crushed toasted cashews, but you could try it with a raw grated carrot salad.

SERVES 2 TO 3

3 to 4 large carrots, preferably purple ones, cut into large chunks or batons

2 tablespoons olive oil or melted coconut oil, divided ✳ 1 to 2 teaspoons maple syrup

1 onion, finely chopped ✳ 1 small red chile, seeded and finely chopped

1-inch piece fresh ginger root, peeled and grated ✳ 2 garlic cloves, finely chopped

½ teaspoon dried red chile flakes, plus extra for sprinkling

¼ teaspoon ground cumin or coriander ✳ ¾ cup split red lentils, rinsed and drained

2½ cups hot Cooked Vegetable Stock (see page 15) ✳ 2 tablespoons cashews

salt and pepper

Preheat the oven to 400°F.

To caramelize the carrots, put them in a bowl and toss with 1 tablespoon of the oil, the maple syrup, and some seasoning to coat. Tip them into a roasting pan and roast in the oven for 20 to 30 minutes, or until tender and golden.

While the carrots are roasting make the soup. Heat the remaining oil in a large saucepan, add the onion, fresh red chile, ginger, and garlic and fry gently for 4 to 5 minutes until softened. Add the chile flakes and cumin or coriander and cook, stirring, for a few minutes.

Add the red lentils and stock. Bring to a boil, then turn the heat down and simmer, partly covered, for 20 minutes, or until the lentils are tender.

Before serving, toast the cashews. Put them in a large, dry skillet and toast over medium heat for 3 to 4 minutes, tossing them in the pan occasionally, until golden all over. Transfer the nuts to a cutting board, let cool, then finely chop.

To serve, ladle the soup into bowls, top with the roasted carrots, scatter with the finely chopped toasted cashews, and sprinkle with chile flakes.

Nutrition tip

Red lentils are a good plant source of iron, and serving them with the toasted cashews adds a second burst of this anemia-protective mineral, too.

A DOLLOP of plain yogurt and a handful of chopped cilantro leaves would also make a great topping.

SERVE with grilled flatbread or naan bread.

ADD some cubes of oven-roasted tofu or grilled eggplant.

USE less stock and serve as a lentil dahl or accompaniment.

BLACK-EYED BEAN CHILE SOUP

This recipe is a combination of chile-flavored greens and creamy-textured black-eyed beans. You can blend everything to make a thick, creamy soup, or stir the whole beans into the blended greens. I've served the soup with a swirl of green herb oil and a cooling dollop of vegan sour cream to temper the heat slightly.

SERVES 3 TO 4

1 cup dried black-eyed beans, rinsed and drained

2 tablespoons olive oil or coconut oil ☀ 1 large onion, finely chopped

2 to 3 garlic cloves, finely chopped ☀ 2 fresh green chiles, seeded and finely chopped

4 to 5 cavolo nero leaves, tough stalks removed and leaves torn into 1-inch pieces

pinch of dried chili powder ☀ 2 large handfuls of baby spinach

3 to 4 scallions, finely chopped ☀ 1 cup hot Cooked Vegetable Stock (see page 15)

1 Little Gem lettuce, finely shredded ☀ salt and pepper

TO SERVE

Raw Sour Cashew Cream (see page 138) ☀ Green Herb Oil (see page 135)

Put the beans in a bowl and cover with plenty of cold water. Let soak overnight, then drain.

Place the beans in a large saucepan, cover with fresh cold water, and bring to a boil, then turn the heat down and simmer, partly covered, for about 1 hour, or until tender. Drain the beans and set aside until ready to use.

Heat the oil in a large sauté pan. Fry the onion, garlic, and green chiles gently until softened.

Stir in the cavolo nero and chili powder, cover, and cook for 5 to 6 minutes until the leaves have wilted. Stir in the spinach and scallions and cook for another few minutes, stirring occasionally, until the spinach has wilted.

Add the stock and lettuce. Blend using a hand-held stick blender, leaving the greens only partly blended if you prefer. Stir in the cooked beans and reheat briefly, if needed, then season to taste.

To serve, ladle the soup into bowls, top with a raw sour cream, and drizzle with herb oil.

Nutrition tip

All the lovely deep greens in this soup make it a good source of iron, vitamin C, and vitamin A.

TRY SERVING with warm corn tortillas and topped with diced avocado.

USE canned black-eyed beans for a quick alternative to dried beans.

SHREDDED ham hock, slow-cooked pork, or crumbled crispy bacon or pancetta also work well in this soup.

SPRING NOODLE SOUP

This simple noodle soup is fragrant and filling without being heavy. It uses translucent, gluten-free rice noodles, which are simmered in a flavorsome broth. Any tender young green vegetables work well as the green element in this soup.

SERVES 2 TO 3

1 teaspoon sesame oil ✳ 2 to 3 garlic cloves, finely chopped

1 small green chile, seeded and chopped ✳ 3 scallions, finely chopped

1-inch piece fresh ginger root, peeled and finely chopped

4 to 5 asparagus spears, woody ends broken off, chopped into 1-inch lengths

½ cup fresh or frozen peas ✳ 1 small handful of monk's beard (agretti) or samphire

2½ cups hot Cooked Vegetable Stock (see page 15)

3 bundles of rice noodles, about 8 oz total weight

juice and finely grated zest of 1 lime ✳ 1 tablespoon hoisin sauce ✳ salt and pepper

TO SERVE

1 teaspoon black sesame seeds

1 small handful of pea shoots or fragrant herbs, such as cilantro

Heat the sesame oil in a large saucepan or sauté pan, add the garlic, chile, scallions, and ginger and fry gently until softened.

Add the asparagus, peas, monk's beard, and stock. Let simmer, covered, for 5 to 10 minutes until the vegetables are tender.

Add the rice noodles, stir, and let simmer for a further 3 minutes or until the noodles are cooked and tender. Stir in the lime juice and zest and hoisin sauce. Season to taste with salt and pepper.

To serve, ladle the soup into bowls, sprinkle with the black sesame seeds, and scatter with the pea shoots or herbs.

Nutrition tip

Soluble and prebiotic fibers in the peas and asparagus make this light soup a good one for the health of your digestive tract and cardiovascular system.

ADD stir-fried marinated mushrooms, tofu, or shredded cooked chicken.
CRUSHED dry-roasted or toasted peanuts would also make a good crunchy topping.

ALPHABET SOUP

You can make this soup using dried alphabet pasta but making your own letter shapes is a much healthier option and a great way to encourage kids to eat more of the good stuff! You can add the letters to any soup or salad, or steam them and serve as a side dish. They are best cut from firm raw vegetables, such as sweet potato, carrots, beet, mooli, or jicama.

SERVES 2 TO 3

1 large sweet potato, peeled and thinly sliced into disks

1 large carrot, thinly sliced into disks

1 large raw beet or candy cane beet, thinly sliced into disks

3 cups Quick "No-Recipe" Light Vegetable Stock (see page 16)

1 small handful of chopped mixed herbs, such as parsley, basil, dill, and chives

salt and pepper

Using cookie cutters, cut out alphabet letters from the sweet potato, carrot, and beet disks. Save any leftover scraps to use in a stew, salad, or juice.

Gently heat the vegetable broth and stir in the letters and herbs, reserving a few to garnish. Let simmer for a few minutes to warm everything through then check the seasoning.

To serve, ladle the broth into bowls and scatter with a few extra herbs.

Nutrition tip

This soup provides vitamin A, and the nitrate-rich beet helps opens up blood vessels and reduce blood pressure.

STIR in a handful of finely sliced leafy greens, such as baby kale, spinach or swiss chard, fresh peas, grated carrot, cooked navy beans, or small pasta shapes for a more substantial meal or in place of the alphabet letters.

SHREDDED cooked meat such as chicken or flaked cooked fish would work well, too.

WHITE SPROUTING BROCCOLI SOUP

White sprouting broccoli is such a seasonal treat and tastes far less like cabbage than the purple sprouting variety. If you can't get hold of either, regular broccoli can be used instead. I've used vegan butter to give a more luxurious, creamy taste, but substitute with olive oil, coconut oil, or regular butter, if you prefer.

SERVES 3 TO 4

2 tablespoons vegan butter ❋ 1 small onion, finely chopped

2 zucchini, coarsely chopped ❋ 2 large bunches of white sprouting broccoli, coarsely chopped

2½ cups hot Quick "No-Recipe" Light Vegetable Stock (see page 16)

juice and finely grated zest of 1 lemon ❋ salt and pepper

Heat the butter in a large saucepan, add the onion, and fry gently for a few minutes until softened but not colored.

Add the zucchini and broccoli, cover, and let cook for 5 to 10 minutes until the broccoli starts to wilt.

Pour in the vegetable stock, cover, and let simmer for 15 to 20 minutes until the zucchini and broccoli are cooked. You can keep them slightly al dente, if you prefer.

Remove the pan from the heat and purée or partially blend the soup using a hand held stick blender, or blend in a food processor. Season to taste with salt and pepper.

To serve, ladle the soup into bowls and stir in the lemon juice and zest just before serving.

Nutrition tip

White sprouting broccoli has all the benefits of normal broccoli, so this soup is a good source of folic acid and beta-carotene.

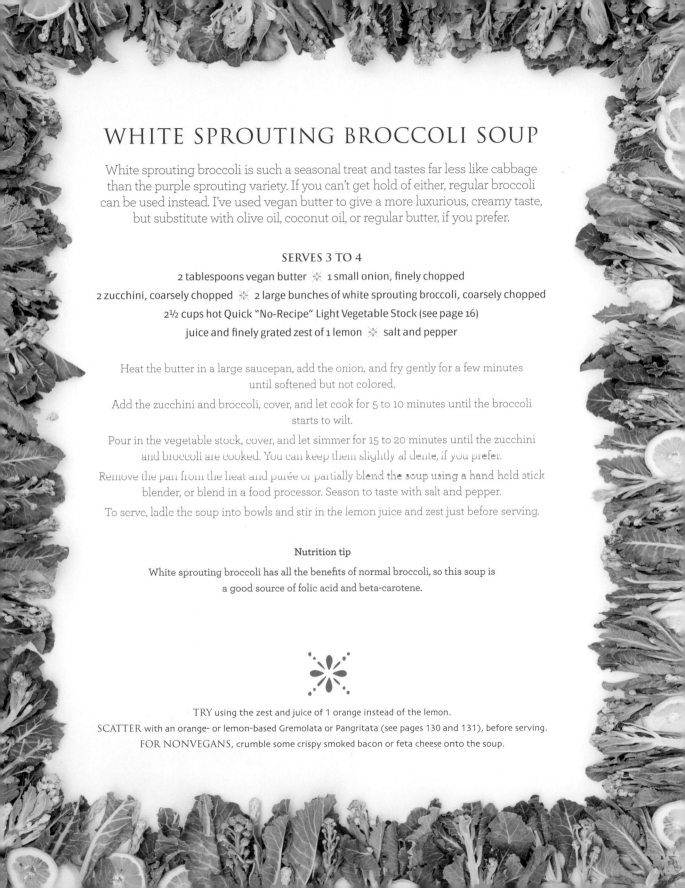

TRY using the zest and juice of 1 orange instead of the lemon.

SCATTER with an orange- or lemon-based Gremolata or Pangritata (see pages 130 and 131), before serving.

FOR NONVEGANS, crumble some crispy smoked bacon or feta cheese onto the soup.

MATZO BALL SOUP

A vegan version of the classic chicken broth with dumplings. Flaxseeds, which act as a binding agent when combined with water, are used instead of eggs in the traditional dumplings. A scattering of fried sage leaves give a delicate savory crunch.

SERVES 2 TO 3
FOR THE VEGETABLE BROTH

1 tablespoon olive oil ✳ 2 garlic cloves, finely chopped ✳ 1 onion, finely chopped
2 scallions, finely chopped ✳ 2 large carrots, finely chopped ✳ 3 to 4 mushrooms, finely chopped
3 celery stalks, finely chopped ✳ 2½ cups hot Cooked Vegetable Stock (see page 15)
1 small handful of flat-leaf parsley, leaves finely chopped
salt and pepper ✳ Crispy Sage Leaves (see page 132), to garnish

FOR THE MATZO BALLS

1½ cups matzo meal or matzo crackers crushed into fine bread crumbs
2 tablespoons ground flaxseeds ✳ 1 tablespoon whole flaxseeds ✳ 3 tablespoons quinoa flakes
1 tablespoon chopped fresh dill ✳ ½ teaspoon onion salt ✳ ½ cup water

First make the matzo balls. Mix together everything except the water in a large bowl, then stir in the measured water and season to taste. Let stand for 5 to 10 minutes to thicken. Stir in extra water, if needed, at this point—you want to achieve a slightly moist but "moldable" consistency.

To shape the matzo balls, place a heaped teaspoon of the mixture in the palm of your hand and roll it into a ball using your other hand. Place the ball on a sheet of nonstick parchment paper and repeat with the remaining mixture. Bring a large pan of salted water to a boil, place the matzo balls in the water, and cook at a robust simmer for 30 to 40 minutes until cooked right through. When cooked, place on a plate lined with paper towels and set aside until required.

While the balls are cooking, make the broth. Heat the oil in a large saucepan or sauté pan, add the garlic, onion, scallions, carrots, mushrooms, and celery and fry gently until softened. Add the stock and simmer for 10 to 15 minutes until the vegetables are just tender. Stir in the parsley and season to taste.

Drop the matzo balls into the broth. Simmer briefly to bring both up to eating temperature.

To serve, ladle the broth into bowls before scattering with a handful of crispy sage leaves.

Nutrition tip

The quinoa and flaxseeds in the matzo balls bump up levels of protein, omega-3, and the mineral magnesium.

FINELY SHREDDED CABBAGE, Swiss chard, and leeks work well in the broth and increase the vegetable content.
GROUND ALMONDS work well in place of quinoa flakes.

ROOT SOUP

This speedy root vegetable soup is made with the same three primary ingredients as the röstis that are served with them. The two recipes start off in the same grated format, so it's easy to make both at the same time.

SERVES 4 TO 6

2 raw beets, coarsely grated ✳ 2 large carrots, coarsely grated

2 large parsnips, coarsely grated ✳ 2 garlic cloves, finely chopped

3½ cups hot Cooked Vegetable Stock (see page 15)

salt and pepper ✳ Root Vegetable Rösti (see page 132), to serve

Simply place all the ingredients, except the rösti, in a large saucepan and bring to a simmer. Cook for 10 to 15 minutes until the vegetables are tender.

Remove the pan from the heat and blend until completely smooth using a hand-held stick blender, or blend in a food processor. Season to taste with salt and pepper.

To serve, ladle the soup into bowls and top each serving with a rösti.

Nutrition tip

This is comfort food without the calories, as well as being a great source of potassium and natural nitrates that will help to keep your blood pressure at a healthy level.

✳

A FEW TABLESPOONS of Raw Cashew Cream (see page 138) or crème fraîche will add a rich creaminess.

COMPLEMENT the flavors of the soup and rösti by scattering it with flaked smoked fish, such as salmon or mackerel. A squeeze of lemon and a sprinkling of fresh dill would taste good, too.

SPEEDY PEA SOUP

This is a super simple, speedy soup that can be ready in 15 minutes. You can blend it completely so it's smooth or leave some peas whole for a little texture. Cooking the garlic first gives it a head start on the peas and tempers its strong flavor. Crisp and crunchy toppings are the perfect contrast to the silky, smooth soup.

SERVES 3 TO 4

4 to 5 garlic cloves, peeled and left whole ❊ 2 cups frozen peas

2 cups hot Cooked Vegetable Stock (see page 15)

2 to 3 tablespoons Raw Cashew Cream (see page 138) or crème fraîche

1 small handful of mint leaves ❊ salt and pepper

TO SERVE

Crispy Sprout Leaves (see page 132) ❊ Savory Granola (see page 131)

Put the garlic cloves in a large saucepan and just cover with cold water. Bring the water to a boil and let simmer for 5 minutes until tender.

Add the peas and stock and simmer for a further 5 to 7 minutes until the peas are just cooked through. Add the cashew cream and mint leaves.

Remove the pan from the heat and blend until silky smooth using a hand-held stick blender, or blend in a food processor. Season to taste with salt and pepper.

To serve, ladle the soup into bowls and top with the crispy sprout leaves and savory granola.

Nutrition tip

Frozen peas contain good amounts of iron and thiamin (a B vitamin that helps to release energy from food) as well as soluble fiber.

ADD diced smoked cooked ham, pancetta, or shredded salami or prosciutto.

USE fresh tarragon, cilantro, or dill as alternatives to the mint.

SERVE as a dip or as a topping for crostini, reducing the quantity of stock to give the soup a thicker consistency.

ROASTED EGGPLANT SOUP

This pale-colored, velvety smooth soup gets its lovely smoky flavor and creamy taste from the roasted and blended eggplants, and can be eaten warm or chilled. Pangritata (see page 131) adds a complementary citrus taste and savory crunch.

SERVES 2

2 eggplants, cut into 1-inch dice ❊ ¼ cup olive oil, divided
1 onion, finely chopped ❊ 3 to 4 garlic cloves, peeled
1¾ cups hot Cooked Vegetable Stock (see page 15)
juice of 1 lemon, plus extra to serve ❊ salt and pepper
Pangritata (see page 131), to serve

Preheat the oven to 425°F, and heat two roasting pans.

Place the diced eggplant in a bowl, toss with 3 tablespoons of the oil until lightly coated, then tip it onto the heated roasting pans. Spread the dice out in a single, even layer. Roast for 20 to 30 minutes until light golden on all sides.

While the eggplant is roasting, heat the remaining oil in a large, deep saucepan, add the onion and garlic, and cook over medium heat until softened but not colored.

When the eggplant is cooked, add it to the pan with the stock, lemon juice, and salt and pepper.

Remove the pan from the heat and purée until silky smooth using a hand-held stick blender. Add more stock, if you prefer a thinner consistency, and additional lemon juice and seasoning to taste.

To serve, ladle the soup into bowls and serve sprinkled with the pangritata and an extra squeeze of lemon juice, if desired. Or, you could drizzle each serving with lemon oil.

Nutrition tip

Nasunin, an anthocyanin found in eggplant, has been shown in laboratory studies to protect the delicate fats in brain-cell membranes.

❋

CRUMBLE feta cheese or crispy fried anchovies onto the soup for an extra flavor boost.
A SPRINKLE of Za'atar (see page 128) or a pinch of smoked paprika is lovely with this soup.
SERVE as a dip by reducing the quantity of water slightly—it's almost like a baba ganoush.
FOR AN EXTRA SMOKY FLAVOR, instead of roasting diced eggplant in the oven, char the whole eggplants under the broiler or on a barbecue, remove the blackened skin, and purée the flesh.

SAVORY OAT SOUP

Not just for breakfast! Rolled oats are a great gluten-free option for thickening soups and stews and can be left whole for a chunky texture or blended in to give a rich, creamy consistency. You can stir the oats into a warm soup and eat immediately, or cook them for longer so they thicken further, or just stir them into a savory broth and let soak in the fridge overnight for a savory porridge to eat in the morning. Here, I've mixed the oats with a quick tomato soup. A green cashew drizzle lifts the flavor and adds a shot of color and chlorophyll.

SERVES 2 TO 3

½ tablespoon olive oil ❋ 1 to 2 garlic cloves, finely chopped

2¼ cups cherry tomatoes, cut in half ❋ 1 small handful of basil leaves

½ teaspoon coconut sugar or sweetener of choice

1 cup regular rolled oats ❋ salt and pepper

Green Cashew Drizzle (see page 137), to serve

Heat the oil in a wide saucepan or sauté pan, add the garlic, and cook gently without browning.

Add the tomatoes, basil, and sugar and cook, covered, for 10 to 15 minutes, stirring occasionally, or until the tomatoes have released their liquid and softened to a pulpy consistency. Season to taste with salt and pepper.

Stir in the oats and add a little water to thin the mixture, if needed. Let simmer for a further few minutes until the oats are warmed through, or cook for longer until the oats are softened and yield a thicker, creamier soup.

To serve, ladle the soup into bowls and add a swirl of the green cashew drizzle.

Nutrition tip

Oats contain the soluble fiber beta glucan, which has been shown to help keep blood cholesterol levels in check.

A GREAT "TRAVELING" SOUP—just place the uncooked oats in a thermos with the warm tomato mixture and let them cook slowly in the liquid until you're ready to eat the soup.

FINELY DICED chorizo or spicy cured meat stirred into this soup will entice nonvegans.

TRY CRUMBLING goat cheese or crispy bacon onto the soup, or serve with a poached or softly boiled egg.

BLUE SPIRULINA SOUP

You'll have noticed by now that I love vibrant, colorful soups. So, to complete the spectrum, here's a soup that's blue. This is a savory soup that's made with healthy raw vegetable and spirulina powder (which is what makes it blue). It is just like a savory smoothie, only it's eaten out of a bowl.

SERVES 2 TO 3

½ head of cauliflower, broken into small florets

1 avocado, cut in half, seed removed, flesh scooped out

1 shallot, coarsely chopped ❋ ⅓ cup cashews

½ small garlic clove ❋ 1 cup coconut water

1 teaspoon spirulina powder ❋ salt and pepper

1 apple, chopped into matchsticks, to serve

Grate or crumble a few of the cauliflower florets into a ricelike texture and reserve to garnish the top of the soup.

Put the remaining cauliflower into a high-speed blender with the rest of the ingredients, apart from the apple, and blend until smooth and creamy.

To serve, pour the soup into bowls and top with the apple and grated cauliflower.

Nutrition tip

Spirulina is a superfood algae and a rich source of plant-based protein, omega-3, vitamins B1, B2, B3, copper, iron, antioxidants, and a whole host of other valuable nutrients. With so many nutrient-packed ingredients in this soup, it's the perfect all-round health tonic.

SERVE CHILLED by placing the soup in the fridge for 2 to 3 hours, or until ready to eat.

YOU COULD USE green spirulina, blue-green algae powder, chlorella powder, or wheatgrass powder as an alternative to the blue spirulina.

DRESS spiralized zucchini or sweet potato noodles with the soup, for a quirky-looking main dish.

RAW BELL PEPPER, ORANGE & TOMATO SOUP

This vibrant, raw, savory soup has a combination of sweet, sour, and spicy flavors. Serve it simply or, as I've shown here, with the addition of orange slices, sourdough croutons (see below), preserved mini bell peppers, and a drizzle of Raw Sour Cashew Cream (see page 138).

SERVES 2 TO 3

3 large red or orange bell peppers, seeded and coarsely chopped

1 small red chile, seeded and coarsely chopped

2¼ cups large chunks of ripe tomatoes

3 large blood oranges, peeled 1¼ cups carrot juice

salt and pepper

Place all the ingredients in a food processor or high-speed blender and blitz until thick and smooth.

To serve, ladle the soup into bowls and serve with your choice of toppings.

Nutrition tip

Brimming with vitamins A and C, this soup makes a really big contribution to topping off your immune defenses. It will help keep your skin vibrant and heathy, too.

TO MAKE THE CROUTONS, fry torn up pieces of sourdough bread in olive oil or butter until crisp and golden,

FOR AN EXTRA-SAVORY FLAVOR, add a small garlic clove before blending. Grate a little orange zest onto the soup before serving for extra zing.

STRAWBERRY SOUP

Chilled strawberry soup is a lovely way to end a meal and it also makes the most of a summertime glut of strawberries. A swirl of sweetened cashew cream gives this sweet soup a luxurious feel and an added creamy texture.

SERVES 2 TO 3

½ lb ripe strawberries ❋ ½ cup coconut water

⅔ cup coconut yogurt ❋ Vanilla Cashew Cream (see page 138), to serve

Wash and hull the strawberries (if you're using organic strawberries reserve the tops to use in a smoothie or juice) and coarsely chop the fruit.

Place the strawberries in a high-speed blender with the coconut water and yogurt and blend until smooth. Cover and chill in the fridge for 2 to 3 hours, or until ready to serve.

To serve, ladle the soup into bowls or chilled glasses and add a swirl of cashew cream on top.

Nutrition tip

Strawberries provide more vitamin C than oranges, and they're also packed with heart-friendly anthocyanin antioxidants and folic acid.

FREEZE in ice-pop molds or a freezerproof container for a healthy ice cream.

ADD a few ice cubes to the soup, or a swirl of balsamic vinegar to enhance the flavor of the strawberries.

A GOOD VEGAN ALTERNATIVE to traditional yogurt is coconut yogurt, but if you eat dairy products try Greek yogurt or any thick, mild, plain yogurt.

SPARKLING PINEAPPLE SOUP

This can be served as a palate cleanser between courses, as you would a sorbet, or as a sweet, refreshing end to a meal. Serve in chilled glass cups, cocktail glasses, or, if you keep the mixture thick, in delicate glass bowls with a spoon. The saffron powder enhances the golden color of the fruity soup, but don't add too much of it.

SERVES 3 TO 4

½ pineapple, peeled, cored, and chopped into chunks

1-inch piece fresh ginger root, peeled and chopped

splash of coconut water (optional)

1¼ cups Prosecco, Champagne, or sparkling wine

few pinches of saffron powder, to decorate

Run the pineapple and ginger through a juicer if you want a thin liquid, or blend in a high-speed blender with a splash of coconut water or water to give a thick consistency similar to a smoothie.

To serve, pour 2 tablespoons of the pineapple and ginger mixture into each glass and top off with Prosecco, Champagne, or sparkling wine. Finally, sprinkle with a tiny pinch of saffron and swirl it into the foamy top.

Nutrition tip

Fresh pineapple contains a compound called bromelain, which is thought to act as a natural digestive aid.

FREEZE the pineapple and ginger mixture to make a sorbet, granita, or alcoholic ice pops.
FOR A lovely tropical, nonalcoholic drink, substitute coconut water for the Prosecco.
SERVE poured over a fresh fruit salad for a sweet, bubbly dessert.

CHILLED FRUIT SOUP

A sweet, pink soup that is best served well chilled. If you haven't got time to refrigerate it then just add a few ice cubes when serving. The frozen berries provide a pretty frosted decoration and will also help chill the soup. For a decadent breakfast, stir in a glass of chilled Champagne or Prosecco to start your morning with a sparkle.

SERVES 2 TO 3

1¾ cups blackberries ❋ 1⅓ cups blueberries, divided

2 cups raspberries, divided ❋ 1¼ cups red currants, divided

1 large mango, peeled, seed removed, flesh diced

2 to 3 peaches, stones removed, flesh quartered

3 to 4 large oranges, peeled and segmented ❋ 1 cup coconut water

Open-freeze all of the blackberries and half of the blueberries, raspberries, and red currants, so they are completely frozen ahead of serving the soup.

Place the mango, peaches, and orange segments in a high-speed blender with the remaining unfrozen blueberries, raspberries, and red currants and the coconut water, then blend until silky smooth. Taste and adjust for sweetness and consistency, thinning with a little extra coconut water if necessary. Chill for 2 to 3 hours in the fridge, or until ready to serve.

To serve, pour the soup into chilled bowls and decorate with the frozen berries.

Nutrition tip

To keep our brains healthy and protect against cognitive decline, it's suggested that we consume some purple or red berries every day. This chilled soup is one very delicious way to do just that.

FOR A SUPERFOOD BOOST, stir in 1 tablespoon acai berry powder or lucuma fruit powder.

A GREAT DESSERT when served with thick, whipped Raw Almond Yogurt (see page 137) delicately scented with orange zest, and flavored with a dash of Orange Blossom Water (see page 139).

USE AS A BASE for smoothies and sorbets, or blend with nut milk or cream and then freeze to make a healthy ice cream.

CHILLED PERSIAN YOGURT SOUP

This is a lovely light soup that can be made sweet or savory. I've used a homemade sweetened Raw Almond Yogurt (see page 137), but you can substitute it with a ready-made vegan or dairy yogurt, sweetened or not. I've topped the soup with fragrant herbs, flowers, and nuts, which can also be stirred into the soup and left to infuse their flavor for 2 to 3 hours, or overnight in the fridge if more convenient.

SERVES 2 TO 3

2 cups Raw Almond Yogurt (see page 137) or yogurt of choice

1 to 2 tablespoons Orange Blossom Water or Rose Water (see page 139)

1 handful of ice cubes ❄ 1 to 2 teaspoons maple syrup or sweetener of your choice (optional)

TO SERVE

1 tablespoon pistachios, coarsely chopped ❄ ¼ teaspoon pink peppercorns, crushed

1 tablespoon finely chopped fragrant herbs, such as dill, mint, or fennel fronds

1 tablespoon fresh or dried edible rose petals, or other fragrant edible flowers

Place the yogurt, orange blossom water or rose water, ice, and maple syrup, if using, in a high-speed blender and blitz until smooth.

To serve, pour the soup into chilled bowls and scatter with the pistachios, peppercorns, herbs, and flowers.

Nutrition tip

This is a rich source of calcium (particularly if made with dairy yogurt). Using maple syrup keeps the glycemic index (rate at which it raises blood sugar) healthily low.

FREEZE the soup into ice-pop molds for a creamy frozen treat, or use for the base of a smoothie.

GOLDEN RAISINS would be a nice addition to this soup.

FOR A SAVORY VERSION, use unsweetened yogurt and flavor with herbs, such as sage, thyme, cilantro, chives, oregano, and rosemary, as well as spices including Za'atar (see page 128), sumac, or garam masala. Cucumber, chile, pine nuts, or walnuts are also good additions to a savory variety.

CHILLED SWEET YOGURT SOUP

This sweet, vibrant soup is great served chilled as a dessert, and the tartness of the raspberries and yogurt set off the natural sweetness of the strawberries. I've used homemade almond yogurt, but coconut yogurt, or any other dairy or vegan alternative would be suitable.

SERVES 3 TO 4

3¼ cups raspberries ✳ ⅔ cup chilled coconut water

1⅓ cups hulled, halved strawberries

1 cup chilled Raw Almond Yogurt (see page 137), divided

1 small handful of edible flowers, such as violets, borage, fuchsias, marigolds, or primroses, to decorate

Place the raspberries and coconut water in a high-speed blender or food processor and blend to a thick purée. Transfer to a bowl and set aside.

Place the strawberries in the blender with half of the almond yogurt and blend to make a thick pale pink "soup."

To serve, pour the strawberry soup into individual bowls, then add the raspberry purée and the remaining raw almond yogurt and swirl together to make a decorative marbled pattern on the top. Decorate with a few edible flowers, just before serving.

Nutrition tip

Berries such as raspberries and strawberries are rich in anthocyanins, thought to offer protection against cardiovascular disease and cognitive decline.

FREEZE the "soup" in ice-pop molds or in a freezerproof container to make a healthy ice cream. You can layer the different colors (by freezing after pouring in each layer) to create striped ice-cream pops.

USE as a base for a smoothie.

POUR over a bowl of fresh or frozen berries, such as strawberries, raspberries, blueberries, and red currants, for a type of sweet fruit "stew."

SCATTER with a handful of chopped nuts or flaked coconut, or swirl in a dollop of raspberry chia jam.

CHOCOLATE PUDDLE SOUP

When I was young, my best friend's mother would make us something very similar to this as a treat, except her version was laden with white sugar. This recipe is based on much healthier ingredients, including avocado, frozen bananas, and raw cacao powder. Thin the mixture with extra coconut water if you want a drinkable sweet soup, otherwise serve in bowls as a dessert to eat with a spoon.

SERVES 3 TO 4

2 bananas, peeled, chopped into chunks, and frozen

1 large ripe avocado, cut in half, seed removed, flesh scooped out

2 to 3 tablespoons raw cacao powder ❋ ½ cup coconut water

1 teaspoon maple syrup, date paste, or sweetener of choice (optional)

TO SERVE

sliced strawberries ❋ pomegranate seeds

cacao nibs ❋ freeze-dried raspberry pieces

Put the frozen bananas into a food processor or high-speed blender with the avocado, cacao powder, and sweetener, if using, and blend to a smooth, thick consistency. Thin the mixture with extra coconut water, if too thick, then let chill in the fridge until ready to serve.

To serve, pour or spoon the soup into bowls and decorate the top with sliced strawberries, pomegranate seeds, raw cacao nibs, and freeze-dried raspberry pieces.

Nutrition tip

With very little added sugar, you can enjoy this chocolate treat guilt-free. It's a good source of potassium and monounsaturated fats.

TOP with chopped nuts, chia seed jam, or coconut cream instead.
A PINCH of dried chile flakes adds a spicy hit.
BLEND in 1 to 2 tablespoons almond butter (or other nut butter) for an added protein boost.
FREEZE to make a healthy chocolate ice cream.

FRUIT "BONBON" SOUP

Instead of candy confectionery, these "bonbons" are made of fresh fruit and are a
great way to encourage kids to find the fun in fruit and enjoy its natural sweetness.
Use as many brightly colored fruits as you can find; I've also used a small amount of
beet to give a beautiful magenta color to the soup (you can't detect the taste at all).
If you can find pink-fleshed dragon fruit by all means use that instead of the beet.

SERVES 4 TO 6

FOR THE SOUP

2 frozen bananas (you can use unfrozen ones, but frozen give a texture like ice cream)

2 large pears, cored and cut into large chunks

1 pineapple, peeled, cored, and cut into large chunks

1 thumb-sized piece of raw beet, peeled ❄ 1 cup coconut water

FOR THE "BONBONS"

1 small papaya, cut in half and seeded ❄ ½ small watermelon

1 dragon fruit, cut in half ❄ 2 kiwi fruit, cut in half

6 to 8 physalis (cape gooseberries), outer leaves removed

a few blueberries ❄ a few grapes

To make the "bonbons," using two different sizes of melon baller, scoop out balls of
papaya, watermelon, dragon fruit, and kiwi fruit. Pile the fruit balls along with the physalis,
blueberries, and grapes into a bowl and chill until needed.

To make the fruit soup, place all the ingredients in a high-speed blender and blend until
a smooth, thick consistency.

To serve, pour the soup into bowls and sprinkle with the fruit "bonbons" to decorate.

Nutrition tip

There's no better or more effective way to boost your intake of vitamin C and other antioxidants than
with this delicious fruit medley.

FREEZE the fruit soup to make a healthy ice cream.

THREAD the fruit "bonbons" onto skewers to make mini fruit kebabs.

INSERT toothpicks into the fruit "bonbons" and dunk them into the soup as a kind of fruit fondue.

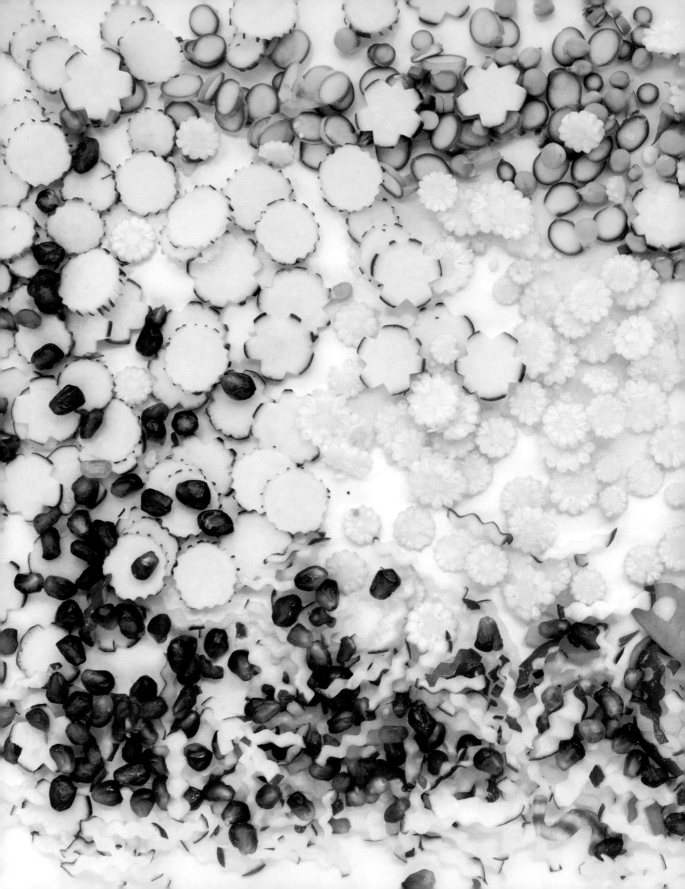

DRY SPRINKLES

1. ZA'ATAR

Sprinkle this Egyptian spice mix onto soups, stews, and cooked vegetables. It also makes a great flavoring for marinades and dressings. You could add other flavorings, too, including dried lemon zest and fennel pollen. Or, if you're planning on eating the za'atar immediately, make it with fresh herbs instead of dried.

2 tablespoons dried herbs, such as thyme, oregano, and marjoram

2 tablespoons toasted sesame seeds ❋ 2 teaspoons sumac

½ teaspoon sea salt

Crumble the dried herbs into a bowl, add the rest of the ingredients, and mix together. If you want a finer blend, process the mixture in a coffee grinder or spice mill, or in a high-speed blender. Store in an airtight container for up to 2 months.

2. DUKKAH

This aromatic North African dry spice mix is made from toasted nuts, seeds, and spices and is great mixed with olive oil as a dip, sprinkled onto cooked vegetables, soups, stews, rice, or lentils, or added to salad dressings. It can also be used to flavor a yogurt marinade.

1 teaspoon hazelnuts ❋ 2 teaspoons sunflower seeds

2 teaspoons coriander seeds ❋ 1 teaspoon fennel seeds

1 teaspoon black onion seeds ❋ ½ teaspoon paprika

⅓ cup Spiced Roasted Chickpeas (omit the spices, see page 134)

salt and pepper

Gently toast the nuts and seeds (except the black onion seeds) in a large, dry skillet until lightly golden, about 2 to 3 minutes. Set aside to cool, then season to taste with salt and pepper.

Place all the ingredients in a food processor and pulse briefly into a coarse, gritty mixture. You can continue to process it into a more finely powdered nutty spice mixture, if you prefer.

Store in an airtight container for up to 1 month.

3. PANCH PHORAN

Made with whole spices, this Indian spice mix is really easy to put together with equal quantities of just five ingredients. It gives a wonderful taste and aroma to any dish requiring curry-type flavors. It's also great sprinkled onto roasted vegetables or crushed and mixed with oil as a dip for bread, or stirred into yogurt as a marinade.

1 tablespoon fenugreek seeds ❋ 1 tablespoon fennel seeds

1 tablespoon black onion seeds ❋ 1 tablespoon nigella seeds

1 tablespoon cumin seeds

Mix the seeds together and store in an airtight container for up to 2 months.

4. GARLIC SALT

Watch this become a favorite kitchen condiment and handy instant flavor booster, minus the nasties, such as anticaking agents, often found in ready-made varieties.

10 to 12 garlic cloves, peeled and left whole

1½ cups sea salt

Preheat the oven to 150°F or as low as your oven will go.

Add the garlic and salt to a food processor and process until the garlic is finely ground. Spread the mixture out onto a large baking pan lined with parchment paper.

Place in the oven for 1 hour, or until completely crisp and dry, but don't allow the mixture to brown.

Break the salt mixture into pieces and blitz in a food processor (make sure the food processor is clean and dried thoroughly first) until the salt has a very fine, gritty texture.

Store in an airtight container for 2 to 3 months.

5. POPPED PUMPKIN SEEDS

Dried pumpkin seeds are really easy to pop. You could flavor them with extra seasonings, such as ground spices, garlic, and herbs. Just mix the seeds with a little oil and combine with the pumpkin seeds before toasting.

¼ cup dried pumpkin seeds from a package

salt and pepper

Heat a large, nonstick sauté pan over medium-high heat and add the pumpkin seeds. Cover with the lid and cook for 3 to 4 minutes until the seeds begin to pop. If you agitate the pan while cooking, the seeds will cook more evenly and it will help them pop. Tip the seeds onto paper towels and season.

Once cool, store in an airtight jar for up to 2 weeks.

... OR TRY ROASTED PUMPKIN SEEDS

Save your fresh pumpkin seeds to roast and scatter onto a soup or salad, or to enjoy as a snack.

seeds from 1 pumpkin

1 to 2 tablespoons olive oil or melted coconut oil

flavoring of choice, such as dried chile flakes, ground cumin, fennel seeds, curry powder, tomato powder, onion salt, paprika, maple syrup, citrus zest, finely chopped rosemary, or finely grated Parmesan

salt and pepper

Preheat the oven to 375°F.

Clean the seeds by removing any attached flesh or membrane and rinse under cold running water. Drain well in a sieve, tip onto paper towels, and pat dry.

Add the seeds to a bowl and pour the oil onto them. Add your flavoring of choice, season to taste with salt and pepper, and stir to coat.

Spread out the seeds in a single layer on a baking pan and roast for 5 to 10 minutes until the seeds are lightly golden.

When roasted, tip the seeds onto paper towels and sprinkle with a little extra salt, if desired.

Let cool and use immediately or store in an airtight jar for up to 2 weeks.

6. POPPED SAVORY QUINOA

Popped quinoa can be flavored to make a savory—or sweet—sprinkle. No boiling required. Simply cook the quinoa in a dry pan until popped and puffed up.

1 cup quinoa

flavoring of choice, such as nutritional yeast flakes, ground turmeric, ground cumin, paprika, or dried herbs

2 to 3 tablespoons nuts or seeds, such as cashews, sunflower seeds, sesame seeds, or pumpkin seeds

salt and pepper

Heat a large, nonstick sauté pan over medium-high heat and add enough quinoa to cover the bottom of the pan in a thin, single layer. Cover with the lid. (You will need to cook the quinoa in batches.)

Lower the heat to medium and cook for 5 to 6 minutes. Shake the pan occasionally, until the quinoa pops and puffs up.

Transfer the popped quinoa to a bowl, add your choice of flavoring, and season to taste with salt and pepper. Repeat with the remaining quinoa and flavorings. Let cool.

Toast the nuts and seeds in the pan for 2 to 3 minutes, tossing the pan occasionally, until starting to color. Let cool then combine with the popped flavored quinoa.

Store in an airtight jar for up to 2 weeks.

7. GREMOLATA

Typically made with three ingredients (lemon, garlic, and parsley), gremolata adds an instant brightness to any dish. Especially lovely with steamed green vegetables or on pasta.

finely grated zest of 1 lemon

1 small handful of parsley leaves

1 garlic clove, minced or grated

Stir all the ingredients to combine. Use immediately or store in an airtight container in the fridge for up to 1 week.

8. SAVORY GRANOLA

Not just for breakfast! This savory version is oat-free, but a handful of oats wouldn't go amiss. You could also blitz the granola in a food processor for a finer sprinkle, if preferred.

9oz mixed nuts and seeds, such as pumpkin seeds, sesame seeds, walnuts, hazelnuts, pecans, and sliced almonds

2 tablespoons ground flaxseeds or chia seeds

2 teaspoons ground spices, such a paprika, garam masala, chili powder, cumin, coriander, or mustard seeds

2 tablespoons olive oil or melted coconut oil

3 tablespoons water ❄ salt and pepper

Preheat the oven to 350°F.

Mix the dry ingredients in a large bowl and season to taste. Add the oil and measured water and stir to combine.

Spread the mixture onto 2 baking pans in a thin, even layer. Bake for 15 to 20 minutes until lightly golden and crispy. You may need to stir it once or twice during baking.

Transfer the pans to a wire rack to cool, then crumble the granola to a coarse texture. Use immediately or store in an airtight container for up to 2 weeks.

9. PANGRITATA

Otherwise known as "poor man's Parmesan," this is a mixture of fried bread crumbs, herbs, and garlic. If you don't have bread on hand, dry crackers make a good substitute.

1 small handful of fresh herbs, such as rosemary, sage, marjoram, and thyme, leaves only

1 to 2 garlic cloves, peeled and left whole

3 slices of stale bread (sourdough is ideal)

1 tablespoon olive oil ❄ finely grated zest of 1 lemon

salt and pepper

Place the herbs, garlic, and bread in a food processor and blitz to chunky or fine crumbs, as you prefer.

Heat the oil in a large skillet over medium-high heat. Add the bread-crumb mixture and fry for 3 to 4 minutes, turning often, until golden and crisp.

Tip onto paper towels, then mix in the lemon zest and season to taste. Use immediately or store in an airtight container for up to 1 week.

DEHYDRATED SPRINKLES & POWDERS

You only need a sprinkling of dehydrated ingredients to give a great flavor boost to your cooking, and they can be used whole, crumbled, or ground into powder. An oven set at its lowest temperature does the job as well as a dehydrator.

10. HERB POWDER

Preheat the oven to 150°F or as low as it will go (or follow the instructions for your dehydrator).

Arrange 2 handfuls of tender herb leaves, such as parsley, cilantro, or dill, in a single layer on a wire rack set inside or on top of a baking pan. Place in the oven for 1 to 1½ hours until the herbs are completely dry and brittle.

Grind, in batches, to a fine powder in a spice mill, coffee grinder, food processor, or high-speed blender. Use immediately or store in an airtight container for 2 months. After that, the powder will start to lose its flavor and fragrance.

11. BEET POWDER

Preheat the oven to 150°F or as low as it will go (or follow the instructions for your dehydrator).

Very finely slice 2 to 3 scrubbed raw beets using a mandoline slicer or sharp knife and arrange in a single layer on wire racks set inside or on top of baking pans. Place in the oven for 3 to 4 hours until completely dry and brittle.

Grind and store as for the Herb Powder.

12. CITRUS POWDER

Preheat the oven to 150°F or as low as it will go (or follow the instructions for your dehydrator).

Remove the peel from 2 large oranges using a small sharp knife and taking care to leave as much of the white pith on the fruit as possible.

Place the peel in a saucepan and add cold water to cover. Bring to a boil and cook for a couple of minutes then, using a slotted spoon, lift the peel out of the water. Transfer to a plate lined with paper towels and pat dry.

Arrange the boiled peel in a single layer on a wire rack set inside or on top of a baking pan. Place in the oven for 18 to 24 hours until completely dry and brittle.

Grind and store as for the Herb Powder.

COOKED SPRINKLES

1. CRISPY SAGE LEAVES

These are delicate and crunchy with a mellow, savory taste, and they lack the heavy, camphorous flavor that many people dislike about fresh sage. Great as a snack, or scattered whole or crushed over soups, pasta, salads, or cooked vegetables.

¼ cup sunflower oil ✳ 1 bunch of fresh sage, leaves only

1 teaspoon sea salt flakes

Heat the oil in a large skillet until hot, add the sage leaves, and fry for 2 to 3 seconds until crisp but without coloring. Using a slotted spoon, transfer the leaves to a plate lined with paper towels to drain, then sprinkle generously with salt.

Use the sage leaves immediately or store in an airtight container for up to 1 week.

2. OVEN-BAKED POTATO CHIPS

You can use this method to make other root vegetable chips, including carrots, beets, or sweet or purple potatoes (the latter makes a colorful addition to any dish). Try seasoning the chips with additional flavorings, such as paprika, curry powder, tomato powder, or Cajun spice mix. Purple potatoes lose their color slightly as you cook them but baking them on a low heat will minimize color loss.

4 potatoes, scrubbed ✳ 2 tablespoons olive oil or melted coconut oil ✳ salt and pepper

Preheat the oven to 400°F.

Slice the potatoes very thinly using a mandoline slicer or sharp knife. Toss gently in the oil to coat and season to taste with salt and pepper.

Tip the potato slices onto large baking pans, spreading them out evenly, and bake for 30 minutes, turning them over once, until cooked and crisp.

Spread the slices out on a large piece of nonstick parchment paper or some paper towels and let dry and crisp up further, about 5 to 10 minutes. Sprinkle with extra salt, if you like.

3. ROOT VEGETABLE RÖSTI

I've included polenta to make these rösti extra crispy. You could fry them, but I find baking is less hassle. Also try with potatoes, celery roots, turnips, or sweet potatoes.

2 tablespoons olive oil or coconut oil

1 beet, scrubbed and coarsely grated

2 carrots, coarsely grated ✳ 1 large parsnip, coarsely grated

2 tablespoons polenta ✳ salt and pepper

Preheat the oven to 425°F. Add the oil to 2 large baking pans and place them in the oven to heat up.

Mix all the ingredients together in a bowl and season to taste with salt and pepper.

Form the vegetable mixture into small balls and place them on the hot baking pans. Flatten the balls with a spatula and bake for 20 to 30 minutes, turning them over once, until cooked through, lightly golden, and crispy.

Drian on paper towels and sprinkle with extra salt, if you like, before serving.

4. CRISPY SPROUT LEAVES

Similar in flavor to kale chips, these make a tasty snack and topping. A great way to use up the outer leaves of sprouts.

¾ lb Brussels sprouts, trimmed and outside leaves (about ¼ lb) removed

2 tablespoons olive oil or melted coconut oil ✳ salt and pepper

Preheat the oven to 375°F.

Place the outer leaves from the sprouts in a bowl, toss gently in the oil to coat, and season to taste with salt and pepper.

Tip the leaves onto a large baking pan, spreading them out in an even layer, and cook for 10 to 15 minutes until crisp and golden around the edges.

Transfer to a plate lined with paper towels to drain. Sprinkle with a little extra salt, if liked. These are best served immediately.

5. SPICED ROASTED CHICKPEAS

Roasted chickpeas make a great snack and even better croûtons. These are smoky and spicy with a bit of bite.

2½ cups cooked dried or a 14 oz can chickpeas, well drained

2 tablespoons olive oil or melted coconut oil

1 teaspoon smoked paprika ✳ 1 teaspoon ground cumin

1 teaspoon Garlic Salt (see page 128), optional

few pinches of chili powder ✳ salt and pepper

Preheat the oven to 400°F.

Tip the chickpeas onto paper towels and rub them until completely dry, discarding any loose skins.

Place them in a bowl, add the oil, and sprinkle with the spices and seasoning. Mix gently to coat the chickpeas.

Spread the chickpeas evenly onto large baking pans and roast for 15 to 20 minutes until golden brown and crispy. Eat immediately or store in an airtight container for up to 2 weeks.

6. MARINATED "PANEER" BITES

Tofu absorbs flavors really well so strong flavorings and seasonings are ideal here. These crunchy, chewy nibbles have a distinct cheese flavor, but you can omit the tofu and use paneer.

juice and finely grated zest of 1 lemon

1 teaspoon maple syrup, or sweetener of choice

½ teaspoon garam masala or curry powder

1 teaspoon Garlic Salt (see page 128)

2 teaspoons nutritional yeast flakes

10 ½ oz tofu, drained and patted dry

1 teaspoon olive oil or coconut oil ✳ salt and pepper

Beat together the lemon juice and zest, maple syrup, garam masala, garlic salt, and nutritional yeast flakes then season to taste. Pour the marinade into a shallow dish or resealable plastic bag. Add the tofu and refrigerate overnight.

Drain the tofu, pat dry, and cut into cubes about ½ inch in size.

Heat the oil in a large, nonstick skillet over medium-high heat, add the tofu, and fry until golden brown on all sides.

Tip the tofu onto a plate lined with paper towels to drain and sprinkle with a little extra salt, if necessary, before serving.

7. CAULIFLOWER STEAKS

I've used mini cauliflowers to make these "steaks." If you're using a large cauliflower then it's best to cook the steaks completely in the oven, or sear them first in a skillet until lightly browned and then finish them off in a medium-hot oven. The steaks are lovely brushed with spiced or flavored oil, such as that from a jar of sun-dried tomatoes.

2 mini cauliflowers, outer leaves removed

1 to 2 tablespoons olive oil or coconut oil ✳ salt and pepper

Carefully slice each cauliflower into four vertical slices and keep any bits that break off to cook alongside the steaks— these get extra crispy and are delicious. Season both sides of the steaks with salt and pepper.

Heat the oil in a large sauté pan, add the cauliflower steaks, and fry until browned on both sides. Cover the pan with the lid and cook gently until tender and cooked through. Transfer the steaks to a plate lined with paper towels to drain. Serve warm.

8. SPICED PARSNIP CHIPS

These oven-baked chips are easy to make and can be adapted to any root vegetables, such as carrots, beets, or sweet potatoes. Season with additional flavorings, such as curry powder, tomato powder, or Cajun spice mix, if you like.

2 to 3 large parsnips, scrubbed

2 tablespoons olive oil or melted coconut oil

½ teaspoon smoked sweet paprika ✳ ½ teaspoon ground cumin ✳ salt and pepper

Preheat the oven to 400°F.

Slice the parsnips very thinly using a mandoline slicer or sharp knife. Toss with the oil, paprika, and cumin to coat and season to taste with salt and pepper.

Tip the parsnips onto large baking pans, spreading them out evenly, and bake for 30 minutes, turning them over once, until cooked through and crisp.

Spread out on a large piece of parchment paper or a plate lined with paper towels and let dry and crisp up further, about 5 to 10 minutes. Sprinkle with extra salt, if you like.

DRIZZLES

1. GREEN HERB OIL

A fragrant oil that can be made with any combination of herbs. The more herbs you use, the thicker the oil, almost becoming a paste. Or, for a clear, bright green oil, steep it in the fridge for 2 to 3 days and then strain and discard the herbs. Great for drizzling over soups, pasta, toasted bread, cooked vegetables, or salads. I've added a small green chile and garlic to give the oil some extra oomph.

2 large of handfuls of mixed green herbs, such as cilantro, basil, parsley, and rosemary

1 garlic clove, peeled and left whole

1 small green chile, seeded ❊ ⅔ cup olive oil

Add the herbs (use the tender stems as well but avoid tough rosemary stalks), garlic, and chile to a food processor and pulse briefly until coarsely chopped.

With the motor running, slowly trickle in the oil and process to a thick, smooth, almost pastelike consistency. Pour in extra oil, if you prefer a thinner consistency. Store in a sterilized airtight jar in the fridge for up to 1 week.

2. FRESH HERB PESTO

This is traditionally made in a mortar and pestle by pounding garlic with salt, fresh herbs, and pine nuts and finally stirring in oil and Parmesan, but the method below is much quicker. This is a cheese-free version, but do add a handful of finely grated Parmesan or vegan hard cheese, if you wish.

1 large handful of tender-leaf herbs, such as basil, parsley, mint, dill, tarragon, and/or cilantro

½ cup extra virgin olive oil

1¾ to 2½ oz nuts or seeds, such as pine nuts, almonds, walnuts, pistachios, or sunflower seeds

2 garlic cloves, peeled and left whole ❊ salt and pepper

Add all the ingredients to a food processor and blitz or pulse to a grainy, saucelike consistency.

Season with salt and pepper and add more oil if too thick. Store in a sterilized airtight jar in the fridge for up to 1 week.

3. SRIRACHA SAUCE

This Asian-style, spicy-sweet, hot chili sauce is addictive—before you know it you are adding it to everything! It often contains sugar, monosodium glutamate (MSG), and a handful of other additives; this version avoids them.

½ lb red or green jalapeño peppers

½ lb small red sweet peppers ❊ 6 to 7 garlic cloves, peeled

½ cup apple cider vinegar ❊ 3 tablespoons tomato paste

¼ cup maple syrup, or sweetener of choice

2 tablespoons soy sauce or *nama shoyu* ❊ salt and pepper

Place all the ingredients in a high-speed blender and process to a smooth, thin paste.

Pour the paste into a small saucepan. Heat to simmering point. Cook gently for 10 to 15 minutes until reduced and thickened. Season and adjust the salty, sweet flavors to taste.

Let cool completely and store in a sterilized airtight jar in the fridge for up to 3 weeks.

4. GAZPACHO SALSA

This fresh-tasting salsa is great with the addition of finely chopped chile for a bit of heat, or a few chopped black olives.

¼ cucumber, finely chopped

½ cup finely diced ripe tomatoes

½ red bell pepper, seeded and finely chopped

1 celery stalk, finely chopped

1 small garlic clove, minced

1 scallion, finely chopped

1 small handful of parsley or basil, leaves finely chopped

salt and pepper

Gently mix together all the ingredients in a bowl. Season to taste with salt and pepper, cover, and refrigerate until required. It will keep for 2 to 3 days in the fridge. Mix the salsa again just before serving.

5. RAW ALMOND YOGURT

This plain, creamy yogurt is also lovely with the seeds scraped from half a vanilla bean or a splash of vanilla extract. To use this recipe in savory dishes, simply omit the sweetener.

1¼ cups raw (skin on) almonds

2 cups coconut water

1 tablespoon coconut syrup or maple syrup, or sweetener of choice

½ teaspoon vegan probiotic powder

pinch of sea salt

Soak the almonds in water for 24 hours until softened, then drain and peel off the skins.

Place the soaked almonds with the other ingredients in a high-speed blender and blend on high until smooth and creamy (this may take a while if your blender isn't very powerful).

Pour the almond milk into a bowl or jar (strain first if not completely smooth). Cover with paper towels or a cloth. Let stand at room temperature for 6 to 12 hours until thickened to a consistency similar to yogurt.

Use immediately or keep in the fridge in an airtight container for 5 to 7 days.

6. GREEN CASHEW DRIZZLE

Swirl this green drizzle onto soup or a vegetable dish, or use it to dress a salad. Blend in ½ small garlic clove for a garlic mayo-type sauce, or ½ green chile for a spicy kick.

¾ cup cashews

1 small handful of mixed greens and herbs, such as parsley, mint, pea shoots, spinach, and basil, leaves coarsely chopped

1 scallion, coarsely chopped

juice and finely grated zest of 1 lemon

salt and pepper (to taste)

Soak the cashews in water for at least 1 hour until softened, then drain.

Place the soaked nuts in a high-speed blender with the other ingredients and add just enough water to cover. Blend on high until smooth and the consistency of light cream (this may take a while if your blender isn't powerful). Season to taste.

Use immediately or keep in the fridge in an airtight container for 2 to 3 days.

7. MACADAMIA CREAM CHEESE

Soaked macadamia nuts blend easily to form a surprisingly good mild-tasting vegan "cheese," which is similar in texture to a crumbly goat cheese. It can be flavored with herbs, garlic, or spices, such as paprika and Za'atar (see page 128). This recipe makes a cheese ball, but you could form it into a log shape or small balls and then roll them in the flavoring, crushed nuts, or seeds.

½ lb shelled macadamia nuts

1 to 1¼ cups water

2 tablespoons melted coconut oil

1 teaspoon vegan probiotic powder

pinch of sea salt

Soak the macadamia nuts in water for 3 to 4 hours until softened, then drain.

Place the soaked nuts in a high-speed blender with the measured water and coconut oil. Blend on high until thick, smooth, and creamy (this may take a while if your blender isn't very powerful).

Pour the macadamia milk into a bowl or jar (strain it first if not completely smooth) and cover with paper towels or a cloth. Let stand at room temperature for 6 to 12 hours (depending on how warm the environment is) until thickened to a consistency similar to yogurt.

Strain the mixture through a nut-milk bag or cheesecloth-lined sieve set over a bowl. Let drain, pressing it down occasionally to extract as much liquid as possible, until the texture of a crumbly goat cheese.

Remove the nut cheese from the bag or cheesecloth and use immediately or keep in the fridge in an airtight container for up to 1 week.

OTHER STOCKS, SAUCES & LIQUIDS

PASSATA (NOT SHOWN)

Need to use up a glut of tomatoes? This is an ideal base for a quick soup or stew. Thinned-down passata makes an almost instant gazpacho as well as the perfect Bloody Mary base.

1 tablespoon olive oil

1¾ lb ripe tomatoes, coarsely chopped

4 to 5 garlic cloves, finely chopped ❈ ½ teaspoon sugar

salt and pepper

Heat the oil in a large saucepan and add the tomatoes and garlic. Cover with the lid and cook gently for 10 to 15 minutes until the tomatoes have softened and released their liquid.

Add the sugar, season well, and let simmer, uncovered, for a further 10 to 15 minutes until reduced and thickened.

Let cool slightly, then press the sauce through a fine sieve—you should be left with a smooth, thick pulp. You could also blend the sauce at this point but the passata will be thicker.

Store in an airtight container in the fridge for up to 1 week, or freeze for up to 1 month.

1. VEGAN DASHI

Traditionally, the Japanese stock dashi uses kombu (seaweed) and bonito (tuna) flakes. This vegan version uses dried shiitake mushrooms and kelp powder to give a similar umami flavor.

1 quart water ❈ 2½oz dried shiitake mushrooms

1 to 2 teaspoons kelp or kombu powder

Pour the water into a large saucepan. Heat until warm.

Put the mushrooms in a large bowl and add the warm (not hot) water. Soak for 3 to 4 hours, then strain the mushrooms (keep them to use in a soup) and reserve the mushroom stock.

Whisk the kelp or kombu powder into the mushroom stock until dissolved. Strain through a very fine or cheesecloth-lined sieve to remove any grit.

Store in an airtight container in the fridge for up to 1 week.

2. RAW CASHEW CREAM THREE WAYS

Most types of nut can be transformed into a raw vegan cream, but if you're not using cashews you'll need to soak them for longer—up to 24 hours—to achieve a similar smooth and creamy consistency.

This yields a thick consistency like heavy cream. If you require a thinner cream, just add more liquid such as water, coconut water, or lemon juice.

¾ cup cashews ❈ ½ cup water

pinch of sea salt

Soak the cashews in water for at least 1 hour until softened, then drain.

Place the soaked nuts in a high-speed blender along with the water and salt and blend on high until the mixture is smooth and the consistency of heavy cream (this may take a while if your blender isn't very powerful).

Use immediately or keep in the fridge in an airtight container for 2 to 3 days.

Variations:
VANILLA CASHEW CREAM

To make a sweetened vanilla version, use coconut water instead of plain water, and add 1 teaspoon maple syrup or sweetener of choice, and the seeds of ½ vanilla bean (or ½ teaspoon vanilla extract) to the blender with the soaked cashews. Continue with the recipe as described, above.

SOUR CASHEW CREAM

To make a vegan sour cream, add 1 tablespoon lemon juice, 1 teaspoon finely grated lemon zest, and 1 teaspoon raw apple cider vinegar to the blender with the soaked cashews. Continue with the recipe as described, above.

3. ORANGE BLOSSOM OR ROSE WATER

It's easier to get hold of beautifully fragrant rose petals to make a floral water than it is to obtain fresh orange blossoms. However, whichever one you use make sure that the flowers haven't been sprayed with chemicals.

This recipe makes a delicately flavored and fragrant infused water. It is not as strong as ready-made versions, so you may need to increase the amount you use. Distilled water can be bought in most drugstores or pharmacies.

2 handfuls of untreated orange blossoms or rose petals

about 1 cup distilled water

Pick the flowers early in the day and wash thoroughly in cool water to remove any dirt. Separate the petals and dry thoroughly, then crush using a mortar and pestle.

Place the crushed petals in a large jar, add the distilled water to cover, and seal with a lid. Place in a sunny position for 5 to 7 days or until the water becomes infused with the flavor and fragrance of the petals. When ready, strain and bottle in sterilized jars. Store in a cool, dark place for 1 to 2 weeks.

4. COCONUT MILK

You can use either fresh or dried coconut, but fresh will give a better flavor. The flesh of a young coconut is softer and blends more easily, but all options yield a plausible and healthier alternative to canned coconut milk.

1 fresh coconut, halved, reserving the water, or 2½ cups unsweetened dried shredded or desiccated coconut

1¼ to 2 cups cold water

If using fresh coconut, cut the flesh away from the shell and put it into a high-speed blender with the coconut water and the lesser amount of measured water. Blend to a pulp, adding extra water if the milk is too thick, or if your blender struggles.

If using dried coconut, use hot water rather than cold because it helps soften and rehydrate it. Put the dried coconut into a high-speed blender with the greater amount of measured water. Blend to a pulp, adding extra water if the milk is too thick, or if your blender struggles to process the mixture.

Pour the coconut milk into a nut-milk bag or a cheese-cloth-lined sieve set over a bowl. Drain, squeezing the pulp to extract all the liquid. Discard the dry pulp or use as body scrub.

Store in an airtight container in the fridge for up to 1 week.

INDEX

agretti (monk's beard) 71, 94
almonds:
    Beet & Barberry Soup 56
    Chilled Persian Yogurt Soup 119
    Chilled Sweet Yogurt Soup 120
    Fresh Herb Pesto 135
    Granola 131
    Raw Almond Yogurt 137
apple 109
asparagus:
    Asparagus & Fennel Soup 53
    Spring Noodle Soup 94
    Spring Vegetable Soup 71
    Super-Greens Soup 29
avocado:
    Alkalizing Green Soup 47
    Blue Spirulina Soup 109
    Chocolate Puddle Soup 123
    Raw Avocado & Cucumber Soup 61

baby corn on the cob 31
bananas:
    Chocolate Puddle Soup 123
    Fruit "Bonbon" Soup 125
barberries 56
basil:
    Alphabet Soup 97
    Broccoli & Lemon Soup 41
    Fresh Herb Pesto 135
    Fresh Tomato Soup 32
    Gazpacho 63
    Gazpacho Salsa 135
    Green Cashew Drizzle 137
    Green Herb Oil 135
    Hidden Vegetable Soup 67
    Raw Vegetable Stock 16
    Savory Oat Soup 107
    Soupy Salad 35
    Three Tomato Soup 86
bay leaves 72
bee pollen 29
beets:
    Alphabet Soup 97
    Beet & Barberry Soup 56
    Beet Powder 131
    Fruit "Bonbon" Soup 125
    Root Soup 102
    Root Vegetable Rösti 132
    Soupy Salad 35
    Velvety Beet Soup 23

berry fruits, see under individual type
bisque 7
black beans 72
black-eyed beans 93
black onion seeds 128
blackberries 116
blending 8–9
blueberries:
    Chilled Fruit Soup 116
    Fruit "Bonbon" Soup 125
"bonbons" 125
borage 120
borscht 7
bouillabaisse 6
broccoli:
    Broccoli & Lemon Soup 41
    Quick "No-Recipe" Light Vegetable
        Stock 16
    Spring Vegetable Soup 71
    Super-Greens Soup 29
    White Sprouting Broccoli Soup 99
broth 7
Brussels sprouts, crispy 132
butter, vegan 37, 45, 75, 99
butternut squash:
    Butternut Noodle Soup 64
    Golden Butternut Squash Soup 49

cabbage 16
cacao nibs 123
cacao powder 123
candy cane beet 97
cape gooseberries (psylium) 125
capers 27
carrots:
    Alphabet Soup 97
    Carrot, Couscous & Chard Soup 54
    Carrot, Orange & Cilantro Soup 46
    Cooked Vegetable Stock 15
    Dehydrated Vegetable Stock Powder 17
    Farro & Pink Radicchio Soup 79
    Hidden Vegetable Soup 67
    Matzo Ball Soup 101
    Quick "No-Recipe" Light Vegetable
        Stock 16
    Red Lentil Soup 91
    Root Soup 102
    Root Vegetable Rösti 132
    Soupy Salad 35
    Sunshine Soup 81

Tomato Cauli Rice Soup 51
cashew cream:
    Beet & Barberry Soup 56
    Black-Eyed Bean Chile Soup 93
    Celery Soup 76
    how to make 138
    Leek & Potato Soup 45
    Mixed Mushroom Soup 68
    Pumpkin Soup 42
    sour 138
    Speedy Pea Soup 104
    Strawberry Soup 113
    vanilla 138
    Velvety Beet Soup 23
cashews 130
    Green Cashew Drizzle 107, 137
    Raw Cashew Cream 138
    Red Lentil Soup 91
    Savory Oat Soup 107
    Sour Cashew Cream 138
    Vanilla Cashew Cream 138
cauliflower:
    Blue Spirulina Soup 109
    Cauliflower Steaks 134
    Coconut Cauliflower Soup 83
    Quick "No-Recipe" Light Vegetable
        Stock 16
    Tomato Cauli Rice Soup 51
cavolo nero:
    Black-Eyed Bean Chile Soup 93
    Butternut Noodle Soup 64
    Spiralized Zucchini & Kale Soup 59
celery:
    Carrot, Couscous & Chard Soup 54
    Celery Soup 6, 76
    Cooked Vegetable Stock 15
    Dehydrated Vegetable Stock Powder 17
    Fresh Tomato Soup 32
    Gazpacho 63
    Gazpacho Salsa 135
    Kernel Corn Soup 87
    Matzo Ball Soup 101
    Quick "No-Recipe" Light Vegetable
        Stock 16
    Soupy Salad 35
    Sunshine Soup 81
    Super-Greens Soup 29
    Swiss Chard & Celery Soup 33
Champagne 115

chard:
Carrot, Couscous & Chard Soup 54
Swiss Chard & Celery Soup 33
cheese:
Pangritata 131
Parmesan 130
substitute 134, 137
vegan 37
chia seeds 131
chickpeas:
Creamy Chickpea Soup 27
Dukkah 128
Spiced Roasted Chickpeas 134
Sweet Potato Soup 88
chiles 131
Black-Eyed Bean Chile Soup 93
Green Herb Oil 135
Raw Bell Pepper, Orange & Tomato
Soup 110
Raw Vegetable Stock 16
Roasted Pumpkin Seeds 130
Spring Noodle Soup 94
Sriracha Sauce 135
chives 61, 97
cilantro
Alkalizing Green Soup 47
Carrot, Orange & Cilantro Soup 46
Dehydrated Vegetable Stock Powder 17
Green Herb Oil 135
Raw Vegetable Stock 16
Spring Noodle Soup 94
citrus fruits (see also under individual type),
Citrus Powder 131
coconut:
Coconut Cauliflower Soup 83
Curried Greens & Coconut Soup 20
coconut milk, how to make 139
coconut sugar 107
coconut water:
Chilled Fruit Soup 116
Chilled Sweet Yogurt Soup 120
Fruit "Bonbon" Soup 125
Raw Almond Yogurt 137
Sparkling Pineapple Soup 115
Strawberry Soup 113
coconuts 139
consommé 7
coriander, ground 131
coriander seeds 128
corn:
Confetti Soup 31
Kernel Corn Soup 87
couscous 54
cranberry beans 39
cream, substitute 12 (see also under
individual type)

crème fraîche 68, 76, 104
chips 75, 132, 134
cucumber:
Alkalizing Green Soup 47
Gazpacho 63
Gazpacho Salsa 135
Raw Avocado & Cucumber Soup 61
Watermelon Gazpacho 50
cumin seeds 128, 130, 131, 134
curry leaves 20
curry powder 130

dashi:
how to make 138
Miso Broths 24
dehydrated sprinkles, powders, how to
make 131
dill 16, 17, 97, 101, 119, 135
dragon fruit 125
drizzles 135
Dukkah:
Carrot, Couscous & Chard Soup 54
how to make 128

eggplants 106

fennel 53, 119
fennel seeds 128, 130
fenugreek seeds 128
flaxseeds 101, 131
flower petals 139
flowers, edible 119, 120
fruit:
fresh, see under individual type
fresh vs. dried 12
frozen 123, 125
fuchsias 120

garam masala 131
Garlic Salt, how to make 128
gazpacho 50, 63, 135
ginger root:
Alkalizing Green Soup 47
Curried Greens & Coconut Soup 20
Miso Broths 24
Quick "No-Recipe" Light Vegetable
Stock 16
Raw Vegetable Stock 16
Red Lentil Soup 91
Sparkling Pineapple Soup 115
Spring Noodle Soup 94
gooseberries 125
granola:
how to make 131
Speedy Pea Soup 104
grapes 125

Gremolata 130

hazelnuts 128, 131
herbs (see also under individual type),
Herb Powder 131
hoisin sauce 94
horseradish 56
jalapeños 16, 135
kaffir lime leaves 83
kale:
Alkalizing Green Soup 47
Butternut Noodle Soup 64
Chunky Cranberry Bean & Kale Soup 39
Spiralized Zucchini & Kale Soup 59
Super-Greens Soup 29
kelp 17, 138
kiwi fruit 125
kombu 138

La Residencia 6
leeks:
Butternut Noodle Soup 64
Leek & Potato Soup 45
Mixed Mushroom Soup 68
Quick "No-Recipe" Light Vegetable
Stock 16
Super-Greens Soup 29
lemon grass 35
lemons:
Broccoli & Lemon Soup 41
Gremolata 130
Pangritata 131
Roasted Eggplant Soup 106
White Sprouting Broccoli Soup 99
lentils 91
limes 50, 83, 94
Little Gem lettuce:
Black-Eyed Bean Chile Soup 93
Soupy Salad 35

macadamia nuts:
Golden Butternut Squash Soup 49
Macadamia Cream Cheese 137
Sweet Potato & Pear Soup 37
mango 116
maple syrup:
Butternut Noodle Soup 64
Chilled Persian Yogurt Soup 119
Chocolate Puddle Soup 123
Marinated "Paneer" Bites 134
Raw Almond Yogurt 137
Red Lentil Soup 91
Roasted Pumpkin Seeds 130
Sriracha Sauce 135
Vanilla Cashew Cream 138
marigolds 120

marjoram 16, 67, 86, 128, 131
matzo meal 101
minestrone 7
mint 88, 104, 119, 135, 137
miso, Miso Broths 24
monk's beard (agretti) 71, 94
mulligatawny 7
mushrooms:
  Dehydrated Vegetable Stock Powder 17
  Matzo Ball Soup 101
  Mixed Mushroom Soup 68
  Quick "No-Recipe" Light Vegetable
    Stock 16
mustard seeds 131

nama shoyu 135
navy beans 84
nigella seeds 128
nuts (see also under individual type),
  creams made from 137, 138

oats, rolled, Savory Oat Soup 107
onion salt 101, 130
orange blossom water 119, 139
oranges:
  Carrot, Orange & Cilantro Soup 46
  Chilled Fruit Soup 116
  Farro & Pink Radicchio Soup 79
  Raw Bell Pepper, Orange & Tomato
    Soup 110
oregano 17, 67, 86, 128

Panch Phoran:
  Butternut Noodle Soup 64
  how to make 128
paneer:
  Marinated "Paneer" Bites 134
  Velvety Beet Soup 23
Pangritata:
  how to make 131
  Roasted Eggplant Soup 106
papaya 125
paprika 17, 128, 130, 131, 134
parsley:
  Alkalizing Green Soup 47
  Alphabet Soup 97
  Butternut Noodle Soup 64
  Chunky Cranberry Bean & Kale Soup 39
  Cooked Vegetable Stock 15
  Dehydrated Vegetable Stock Powder 17
  Fresh Herb Pesto 135
  Gazpacho 63
  Gazpacho Salsa 135
  Green Cashew Drizzle 137
  Green Herb Oil 135
  Gremolata 130

Hidden Vegetable Soup 67
Matzo Ball Soup 101
Quick "No-Recipe" Light Vegetable
  Stock 16
Raw Vegetable Stock 16
Soupy Salad 35
Sunshine Soup 81
Super-Greens Soup 29
Swiss Chard & Celery Soup 33
parsnips:
  Golden Butternut Squash Soup 49
  Root Soup 102
  Root Vegetable Rösti 132
  Spiced Parsnip Chips 134
passata:
  Spiralized Zucchini & Kale Soup 59
  Hidden Vegetable Soup 67
  how to make 138
pasta, Hidden Vegetable Soup 67
pea shoots 94, 137
peaches, Chilled Fruit Soup 116
pears:
  Fruit "Bonbon" Soup 125
  Sweet Potato & Pear Soup 37
peas:
  Confetti Soup 31
  Speedy Pea Soup 104
  Spring Noodle Soup 94
pecans 131
peppers, red, bell:
  Fresh Tomato Soup 32
  Tomato Cauli Rice Soup 51
  Watermelon Gazpacho 50
peppers, sweet:
  Dehydrated Vegetable Stock Powder 17
  Gazpacho 63
  Gazpacho Salsa 135
  Raw Bell Pepper, Orange & Tomato
    Soup 110
  Sriracha Sauce 135
  Sunshine Soup 81
pesto:
  Fresh Herb Pesto 135
  Spring Vegetable Soup 71
pho 7
physalis 125
pine nuts 135
pineapple:
  Fruit "Bonbon" Soup 125
  Sparkling Pineapple Soup 115
pink peppercorns 76, 119
pistachios 119, 135
polenta 132
pomegranate seeds 31, 123
Popped Pumpkin Seeds:
  how to make 130

Velvety Beet Soup 23
Popped Savory Quinoa 130
potage 7
potatoes:
  Kernel Corn Soup 87
  Leek & Potato Soup 45
  Oven-Baked Potato Chips 132
  Purple Potato Soup 75
  Spring Vegetable Soup 71
primroses 120
probiotic powder, vegan 137
Prosecco 115
pumpkin seeds 130
  Granola 131
  Pumpkin Soup 42
  Velvety Beet Soup 23
pumpkins:
  Pumpkin Soup 42
  Roasted Pumpkin Seeds 130

quinoa 101, 130

radicchio 88
  Farro & Pink Radicchio Soup 79
  White Bean & Radicchio Soup 84
radish 31
rainbow chard 54
ramen 7
ransoms:
  Purple Potato Soup 75
  Spring Vegetable Soup 71
ras-el-hanout 88
raspberries 116
  Chilled Sweet Yogurt Soup 120
  Chocolate Puddle Soup 123
raw-food diet 6
red currants 116
rice noodles 94
Roasted Pumpkin Seeds, how to make 130
rose water 119, 139
rosemary 130, 131
  Cooked Vegetable Stock 15
  Green Herb Oil 135
  Quick "No-Recipe" Light Vegetable
    Stock 16
  Raw Vegetable Stock 16
  Swiss Chard & Celery Soup 33
rösti:
  how to make 132
  Root Soup 102

saffron 115
sage 86, 131
  Crispy Sage Leaves 132
  Matzo Ball Soup 101
  Three Tomato Soup 86

salsa 63, 135
samphire 71, 94
scallions:
    Asparagus & Fennel Soup 53
    Black-Eyed Bean Chile Soup 93
    Butternut Noodle Soup 64
    Gazpacho Salsa 135
    Matzo Ball Soup 101
    Miso Broths 24
    Spring Noodle Soup 94
seaweed (see also under individual type),
    Miso Broths 24
seeds, see under individual type
sesame seeds 94, 128, 130, 131
shallots 109
soups:
    author's memories of 6
    benefits of 7
    best ingredients for 8
    blending 8–9
    cooking oil for 8, 12
    cooking utensils for 10–11
    defining 7
    finishing touches to 8
    fruit 7, 8 (see also under individual
        type)
    how to serve 9
    savory 7, 8 (see also under individual
        type)
    stocks for 8, 14
    storing 9
soy sauce 135
sparkling wines 115
spices, see under individual type
spinach 71
    Black-Eyed Bean Chile Soup 93
    Green Cashew Drizzle 137
spirulina powder 29, 109
sprinkles:
    cooked 132
    dehydrated 131
sprout leaves 104
sprouting broccoli 99
squashes:
    Butternut Noodle Soup 64
    Golden Butternut Squash Soup 49
    Pumpkin Soup 42
sriracha:
    Broccoli & Lemon Soup 41
    Golden Butternut Squash Soup 49
    Sriracha Sauce 135
stews 7
stocks 8 (see also vegetable stock)
    Cooked Vegetable Stock 15
    powder 17
    Quick "No-Recipe" Light Vegetable

Stock 16
    Raw Vegetable Stock 16
    tips for making 14
strawberries:
    Chilled Sweet Yogurt Soup 120
    Chocolate Puddle Soup 123
    Strawberry Soup 113
sugar snap peas:
    Alkalizing Green Soup 47
    Confetti Soup 31
sumac 27, 59, 67, 128
sun-dried tomatoes, Three Tomato Soup
    86
sunflower seeds 128, 130, 135
sweet potatoes:
    Alphabet Soup 97
    Sweet Potato & Pear Soup 37
    Sweet Potato Soup 88
Swiss chard, Swiss Chard & Celery Soup 33

tahini 88
tarragon 135
thyme 15, 67, 68, 86, 87, 128, 131
tofu 134
tomato powder 130
tomatoes:
    Dehydrated Vegetable Stock Powder 17
    Fresh Tomato Soup 32
    Gazpacho 63
    Gazpacho Salsa 135
    Golden Butternut Squash Soup 49
    Passata 138
    puréed 135
    Raw Bell Pepper, Orange & Tomato
        Soup 110
    Savory Oat Soup 107
    Soupy Salad 35
    Spiralized Zucchini & Kale Soup 59
    Three Tomato Soup 86
    Tomato Cauli Rice Soup 51
turmeric 130

vanilla 113, 138
vegan diet 6
vegetable stock:
    Alphabet Soup 97
    Asparagus & Fennel Soup 53
    Beet & Barberry Soup 56
    Black Bean Soup 72
    Black-Eyed Bean Chile Soup 93
    Broccoli & Lemon Soup 41
    Butternut Noodle Soup 64
    Carrot, Couscous & Chard Soup 54
    Carrot, Orange & Cilantro Soup 46
    Celery Soup 76
    Chunky Cranberry Bean & Kale Soup 39

Coconut Cauliflower Soup 83
    Confetti Soup 31
    Creamy Chickpea Soup 27
    Farro & Pink Radicchio Soup 79
    Fresh Tomato Soup 32
    Golden Butternut Squash Soup 49
    Kernel Corn Soup 87
    Matzo Ball Soup 101
    Mixed Mushroom Soup 68
    Pumpkin Soup 42
    Purple Potato Soup 75
    Red Lentil Soup 91
    Roasted Eggplant Soup 106
    Root Soup 102
    Speedy Pea Soup 104
    Spring Noodle Soup 94
    Spring Vegetable Soup 71
    Sunshine Soup 81
    Super-Greens Soup 29
    Sweet Potato & Pear Soup 37
    Sweet Potato Soup 88
    Swiss Chard & Celery Soup 33
    Velvety Beet Soup 23
    White Bean & Radicchio Soup 84
    White Sprouting Broccoli Soup 99
velouté 7
vinegar:
    apple cider 135
    balsamic 87
violets 120

walnuts 131, 135
watermelon:
    Fruit "Bonbon" Soup 125
    Watermelon Gazpacho 50

yeast flakes 130
yogurt 12
    Beet & Barberry Soup 56
    Chilled Persian Yogurt Soup 119
    Chilled Sweet Yogurt Soup 120
    Raw Almond Yogurt 137
    Strawberry Soup 113
    Velvety Beet Soup 23

Za'atar 128
zucchini:
    Alkalizing Green Soup 47
    Butternut Noodle Soup 64
    Confetti Soup 31
    Dehydrated Vegetable Stock Powder 17
    Hidden Vegetable Soup 67
    Sunshine Soup 81
    Tomato Cauli Rice Soup 51
    White Sprouting Broccoli Soup 99
    Spiralized Zucchini & Kale Soup 59

A Hachette UK Company
www.hachette.co.uk

First published in Great Britain in 2017 by Mitchell Beazley,
a division of Octopus Publishing Group Ltd.
Carmelite House
50 Victoria Embankment
London EC4Y 0DZ
www.octopusbooks.co.uk
www.octopusbooksusa.com

Copyright © Octopus Publishing Group Ltd 2017

Distributed in the US by Hachette Book Group
1290 Avenue of the Americas
4th and 5th Floors
New York, NY 10020

Distributed in Canada by Canadian Manda Group
664 Annette St., Toronto, Ontario, Canada M6S 2C8

ISBN 978-1-78472-234-0

A CIP catalog record for this book is available from the
British Library.

Printed and bound in China

10 9 8 7 6 5 4 3 2 1

Publishing Director Stephanie Jackson
Art Director Yasia Williams-Leedham
Editor Pollyanna Poulter
Copy Editor Nicola Graimes
Nutritionist Angela Dowden
Assistant Production Manager Marina Maher
Photographer Amber Locke   .

AMBER WOULD LIKE TO THANK...

Firstly, I'd like to thank Stephanie Jackson, publishing director
at Octopus books, for giving me the opportunity to write and
photograph my second book and extend my printed "voice"
into the repertoire of soups. As a "veg evangelist" it's wonderful
to have another literary vehicle to share my passion for fruit
and veg and illustrate how delicious and easy it is to "get more
of the good stuff down"!

Secondly, I'd like to thank the amazing support team at
Octopus who have assembled and crafted this book into
what you see today. In particular, art director Yasia Williams
for working her creative magic on the beautiful design and
layout of this book and for her artistic guidance with styling
and photography, and to my editor Polly Poulter for her
endless patience and gracious editing of me and my rambling
manuscript! Thanks also to PR supremos Karen Baker and
Siobhan McDermott, to copy editor Nicola Graimes, and to all
the other troupers who worked so hard on this book as part
of the "Savor" team.

Words cannot express the gratitude I feel to my parents for
raising me to understand the importance of good food, home
cooking, and an appreciation of the beauty of nature. Thank
you to my mother for helping me source crockery and allowing
me to constantly plunder her cupboards for cutlery and props,
and thank you to my father for a never-ending supply of freshly
painted backgrounds, textured surfaces, and my random
requests for spray-painted leaves, fruit, and vegetables!

To my partner Mark for his constant support, encouragement,
and faith in me and for always pushing me to step outside my
comfort zones!

Finally, huge, massive, and timeless thanks to all the people
who support my work and to all my followers on social media,
without whom none of this would have been possible.

Love and veggie blessings to you all x